# RECLAIM JOY

## A GUIDED JOURNAL TO DISCOVER
## SIMPLE PLEASURES EVERY DAY

### EMINE RUSHTON

*Illustrated by Pui Lee*

*Leaping Hare Press*

First published in the UK in 2021 by
*Leaping Hare Press*
An imprint of The Quarto Group.
The Old Brewery, 6 Blundell Street
London, N7 9BH,
United Kingdom
T (0)20 7700 6700
www.QuartoKnows.com

A catalogue record for this book is available from
the British Library.

ISBN  978-0-7112-6173-0

Ebook ISBN 978-0-7112-6174-7

10 9 8 7 6 5 4 3 2 1

Design by Emily Portnoi

Illustrations by Pui Lee

Printed in China

# CONTENTS

## INTRODUCTION
**P6**

# INTRODUCTION

'THE MEANING OF LIFE IS JUST TO BE ALIVE. IT IS SO PLAIN AND SO OBVIOUS AND SO SIMPLE. AND YET, EVERYBODY RUSHES AROUND IN A GREAT PANIC AS IF IT WERE NECESSARY TO ACHIEVE SOMETHING BEYOND THEMSELVES.'

*Alan Watts*

I can remember the exact moment I realised life was not 'working'. I was a sleep-deprived new mother, back at work full time, stuck on a decommissioned train at 11p.m. I was going nowhere. I had inadvertently found myself on a relentless treadmill – commuting at dawn, collapsing at dusk, with (some weeks) barely a moment of deep, restorative rest in between. Like many people, I found myself living for the weekend and holidays, but was often too wired to relax into them. Or I would be so bone-tired that, at the first hint of a holiday, I'd fall ill and end up in bed.

This happened more times than I would like to admit, until it became clear that there was no way I could keep going. But this is no sad story. It is the beginning of the beginning, the realisation that life is of our own making. Even when things feel bleak and challenging, the sun will rise, the clouds will clear, change is always possible . . . inevitable, even. I'd moved too far away from life's golden core – the good, simple, easeful, joyous abundance, freely found, all around. I had forgotten what the world smells like on a crisp autumn day, touched by the first frost, sweetened by windfall apples. I had lost my way – the way I knew by heart as a child – that had me navigating the sky with my eyes, conjuring castles from clouds, delighting in all things new: hungry for more of this rich and delicious life.

So, I moved to a place where those things came a little more easily. A 250-year-old cottage in a quiet village with two shops and a thousand trees. I left my busy magazine job behind, and found a quieter part-time role instead, editing a beautiful independent mindfulness magazine. I started to study plants and herbs. My family and I made space in our lives for a small garden; the sowing, tending, growing and harvesting came to mirror our own lives in so many ways. We sold countless pointless possessions and the no-longer-needed second car. We switched to green energy, invested in a couple of necessary eco appliances and halved our outgoings. We grew our own veg and some fruit. I dusted off my old sewing machine. We foraged and found, we made and mended. Without high overheads and full-time deadlines, we found more breathing space. Even with two children, things started to simplify. All of a sudden, the load shared between myself and my family felt lighter.

Of course, nothing in life is for ever. We may wake up one morning and find ourselves in a world we scarcely recognise. And yet it is not in spite of this uncertainty that we must do our utmost to live as fully and joyfully as we can – it is, rather, because of it. Because the only certainty in our lives is change. Some changes are seismic, others are subtle, but all are felt. We may decide that we cannot live our lives properly until we have the future all figured out – that it is best to sit out the storms and begin our lives afresh only when the clear blue skies reappear. But we could spend a lot of time in the waiting room that way. And at the end of the day all that we ever have is this one present moment – just one at a time – so the very question of where we are going, or from where we have come, is beside the point.

Whenever I begin to feel that I'm not quite right in my self, I always remind myself of that brilliant Alan Watts quote about the meaning of life – simply, to live it. Having felt rather lost for a time, I have come to rely on the making of magic from the most ordinary moments: this is the very best kind of medicine. The pure pleasure of sipping tea made with freshly picked herbs; the curious calm bestowed upon the mind by the silvery moon; the tongue-tickling delight of a tricksy limerick; the transformative joy of giving ourselves permission to be precisely who we are, at any given moment in time. And so, it is in this frame of mind that I give you 365 ways to go about your day with your eyes, hearts and minds wide open to the possibility of a lot more wonder, curiosity, openness and, of course,

 Joy!

# DAWN DELIGHT

## GIVE HAPPINESS A HEAD START

Life is a series of eternal cycles . . . birth to death, new moon to full, sunrise to sunset . . . When we rise each morning, that morning's momentum and energy are defined by the night that came before . . . and, in turn, the flavour of the day ahead is inextricable from the mood of the morning we enter into. Mornings have long been my favourite time of the day. I always set the intention to rise early – with the larks – while all in my household slumber on, oblivious to my quiet joy downstairs, padding barefoot around the garden or curled up under a blanket with a morning cuppa.

There is something so delicious about being up first . . . about moving into the day with a sense of purpose . . . about choosing to seek goodness, nourishment, enjoyment before most others have shaken off sleep; of coming into the day with gentleness: no alarm, no rush, no fuss. When we wake with kindness – giving ourselves enough time to come fully to our senses, nourishing ourselves with a good first meal, hydrating our parched systems with herbal tea or warm water, awakening all of our senses by stepping outside to greet the sun and sky and forgoing the urge to dive immediately into emails and obligations, we dramatically raise the odds of the rest of the day going well. We remind ourselves that we do have a say in how we enter our day. We remember that joy is intrinsic to living and more readily found and felt when not buried beneath a mountain of morning tasks, trials and tribulations. When we peel back the edge of those first moments of each day, we find a window of opportunity . . . a window we get to fill with gentleness and joy.

1 Each morning, before you do anything at all – before you even open your eyes or begin to move – find three reasons to be thankful for this new day. From the song of the birds to the softness of your pillow, hold on to your three reasons until you REALLY feel them. Then, and only then, get ready to wake up and greet the day.

*Make a note of your three reasons here*

1.

2.

3.

2 Different cultures greet the day in different ways, and a simple 'good morning' is a very jolly thing to say each day, when you come to think of it.

*If you could greet the day in your own way, what would you say?*

3 Make a morning steeper: simply pop apple and/or pear slices and a cinnamon stick into a flask of hot water for delicious hydration to comfort you on your way to work. Naturally sweet flavours are soothing; imagine you're replenishing your inner cup as you drink, and take the time to breathe in the fragrant fruit and spice steam with each sip.

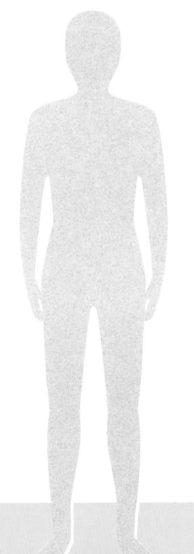

4 Which part of your body needs nourishment today? Scan from the top of your head to the tips of your toes and see where your attention goes.

*Colour the illustration, using a different colour for each body part. Write down what you feel when you focus on each area.*

..................................................
..................................................
..................................................
..................................................
..................................................
..................................................
..................................................
..................................................
..................................................
..................................................
..................................................
..................................................
..................................................
..................................................

5 Greet your morning face in the mirror without fear or judgment. Smile at your reflection, gently lay your hands on your skin and embrace your uniquely natural beauty.

*Sketch your face here, with a big, beatific smile.*

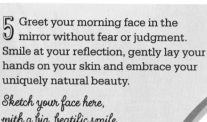

6 Choose **THREE WORDS** that describe who you really are beneath the baggage, obligations, worries and requirements. Who are you at your very core?

*Write your three words here.*

**7** Making the bed in the morning should be a slow ritual, not a rushed chore. Take time to smooth, fold, straighten, shake out and refresh your bed. Place your pillows and blankets just as you like them. What one thing will you leave on your bedside table, ready to welcome you later in the day?

*Squiggle it down here.*

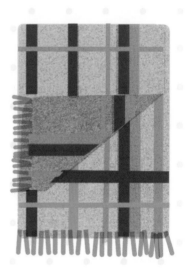

**8** The cheery robin is often the first bird heard at dawn, but did you know it's because robins are nocturnal? They are able to see in very dim light, so they often forage through the night, and when their work is done, they celebrate with a song.

*Sketch a chirpy bird here. What's it tweeting?*

DAWN DELIGHT

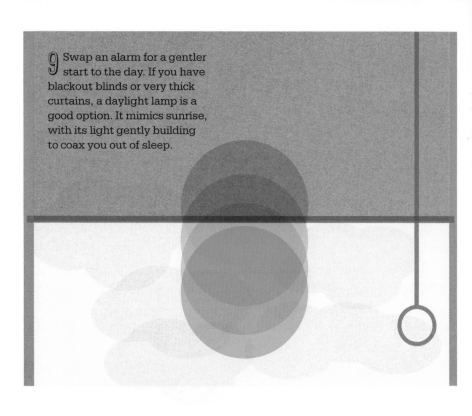

9 Swap an alarm for a gentler start to the day. If you have blackout blinds or very thick curtains, a daylight lamp is a good option. It mimics sunrise, with its light gently building to coax you out of sleep.

10 Pen a short haiku about sunrise – a three-line poem with **FIVE**, then **SEVEN**, then **FIVE** syllables.

*Write your poem here.*

# 11 What's the first thing you see when you wake up in the morning?

*Sketch it here.*

# 12 What's the first thing you WANT to see when you wake up in the morning?

*Sketch it here.*

**13** It's always lovely to rise to the promise of a delicious breakfast. Think of what you'll need to pick up at the shop or market today, in order to enjoy your favourite breakfast tomorrow.

*Doodle your breakfast here, in the bowl below.*

**14** Keep a pot of fresh mint or lemon verbena on your kitchen windowsill. Pop a few fresh leaves into a cup of hot water for a vitalising and aromatic morning brew. Enjoy it somewhere quiet, even if just for a few moments.

**15** Between 6a.m. and 9a.m. sunlight is at its most healing and safe. Your body absorbs precious vitamin D without the risk of heightened UV exposure. Morning sun boosts your happy hormone serotonin and your natural feel-good endorphins, and even lowers blood pressure. Try to reorganize your mornings so that you have time to sit outside for a short spell (weather permitting).

DAWN DELIGHT

16 When you wake up with natural sunlight, the light waves immediately boost your alertness, brain function and mood – ironically the stuff many of us ordinarily drink coffee to 'feel'.

*Take this book outside before breakfast and colour in the sun as it appears in the sky today.*

**17** Morning movement helps wake up your muscles and nerve endings, your brain and joints. Try a short round of sun salutations – gentle yoga stretches that get the blood and heart pumping.

*Decorate this happy yogini, while she salutes the sun.*

**18** The best movement is incidental – when your body does what it needs to do, naturally and instinctively: cleaning, gardening, parenting.

*Make a list of five ways in which you intend to move your body today – ways that will leave you feeling energised, not depleted.*

1.

2.

3.

4.

5.

**19** Everyone should have a good morning playlist. Think about the top ten happiest songs that make you tap your toes, wiggle your bottom and grin from ear to ear. Pop them into a playlist, and whenever your morning feels grey, just press play.

*Write your song titles here.*

**20** Take a picture of a favourite, easily accessible morning view and remember to take three more, one each season. Take the picture from the exact same spot each time so that you can see what has changed and what hasn't.

*Stick all four pictures here, side by side, and note down the changes.*

........................................................    ........................................................
........................................................    ........................................................
........................................................    ........................................................
........................................................    ........................................................
........................................................    ........................................................
........................................................    ........................................................
........................................................    ........................................................
........................................................    ........................................................

**21** Keep a book of short poetry that you love by your bedside. Treat yourself to a poem each morning.

*Write the book title and page numbers down here, with a line or two from each poem, so that you can always find them again in the future.*

........................................................

........................................................

........................................................

........................................................

........................................................

........................................................

........................................................

........................................................

........................................................

**22** Today, try the simple act of counting to ten before allowing an unkind or critical word to leave your lips. Then return to this entry at the day's end. How did it go?

*Jot down your observations.*

........................................................

........................................................

........................................................

........................................................

........................................................

........................................................

........................................................

........................................................

........................................................

........................................................

........................................................

........................................................

**23** Slide a picture of a joyous memory into your bag or purse. Make time to look at it every morning on your way to work. Let the happiness fill you up.

*Write down three more joyous memories for whenever you need a reminder of your blessings.*

1.

2.

3.

DAWN DELIGHT

$2 4$ Overnight oats are the simplest way to prep a delicious breakfast in advance. Simply half-fill a clean jar with oats, cover them with the milk or yoghurt of your choice and add your toppings. Lid on, pop in the fridge. In the morning, stir through, add some fresh fruit on top and you're good to go!

Here are some yummy combinations to inspire breakfast time:

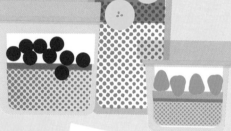

Oats + peanut butter + honey / top with banana

Oats + vanilla + cacao + brown sugar / top with blueberries

Oats + cinnamon + honey / top with strawberries + desiccated coconut

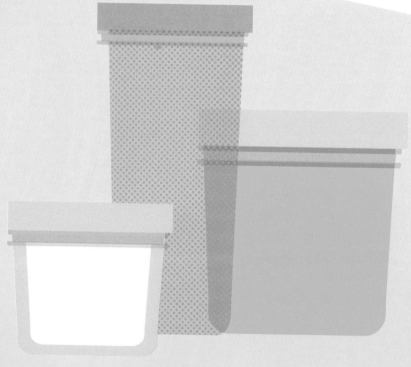

**25** Spiritual teacher **Eckhart Tolle** said that we are more motivated to awaken from a nightmare than from a pleasant dream, and that 'evolution occurs in response to a crisis'. Think about unhelpful patterns or habits you wish to change. What will you do about them?

**26** Which scents make you feel energized and clear-headed? For many people, very green notes, such as basil or rosemary, or citrus notes, such as bergamot and mandarin, are invigorating.

*Add your favourite awakening sprigs and fruits to this bottle of perfume. Can you smell them?*

## CREATE YOUR OWN MORNING MOTTO

**27** A few powerful words that make you feel confident and optimistic. Write them on a piece of paper that you can pop into a small frame to keep by your bedside.

*Write your motto down here, too.*

..................................................................................
..................................................................................
..................................................................................
..................................................................................
..................................................................................
..................................................................................

**28** If the first thing you do when you wake up in the morning is smile, you are already on the right foot. Even if you don't feel like getting up, smiling can help convince your brain that you do. What's the one thing that is guaranteed to make you smile?

*Stick in a picture or prompt here, ready for morning.*

**29** If your system feels sluggish and slow in the morning, enjoy some grated fresh ginger and a slice of lime or lemon in a mug of hot water, at least thirty minutes before breakfast.

**30** Always keep a comfort read by your bed, one filled with uplifting short passages or reflections. Take just one minute each morning to open your book at random and read from it. Make this positive practice part of your purposeful morning routine.

# DAY GLOW

## IT ISN'T WHAT YOU DO, IT'S THE WAY THAT YOU DO IT

We know that life can, at times, feel infeasibly hard. We also know that humans are more easily wired towards negativity than positivity. But this is not a fixed state. The discovery of neuroplasticity has shown that we can all grow new positive neural pathways; we can, literally, think better, brighter and happier. It just takes practice. By putting more of our energy into acknowledging all that is going well in our lives, and reframing how we approach challenges and hardships, we begin to build up a foundation of resilience.

The stronger this foundation becomes, the less likely we are to wobble and fall when facing a new challenge. If we choose to spend time actively seeking out new ways to view the world in a more positive light, the light in our lives will grow exponentially. And if, instead of building up our dread or dislike, we better exercise our equanimity and acceptance, we begin to make more and more positive inroads. One of the most powerful ways we can do this is by paying more attention to the ordinary magic in the world all around us, each and every day – from the distinct movements of plants to the involuntary smiles of strangers. Our daily lives are so full of interesting sounds and sights, yet we are often in such a rush to get to our destinations that we miss the vast majority of these little wonders. This chapter is designed to help you slow down, acknowledge, experience and enjoy the little things a little more. When you do that, you reclaim joy.

**31** What do you hear right now? Which sounds are familiar? And which don't you recognize? What might they be?

*Write down all the layers of sound in your world.*

_____

_____

_____

_____

_____

_____

_____

_____

_____

_____

_____

_____

_____

_____

_____

**32** Think about the last time you felt really free and liquid in your body. What were you doing?

*Jot it down as a 'moving' reminder.*

_____

_____

_____

_____

_____

_____

_____

_____

_____

**33** Choose a colour for the day from these beautiful ink blots. As you go out and about, keep this colour in your mind. See if you can spot things that are the exact same colour. When you come home, jot them down onto your chosen blot. Choose a different colour next time, and the next, until you have completed the page.

DAY GLOW

**34** When we listen to classical music, the mind fills in the stories behind the notes. Listen to some classical music that you are not already familiar with and let your imagination take a ride.

*Write your story down here.*

**35** Smell is one of the most powerful senses. A single sniff, and you're transported back to a summer holiday, a specific moment in childhood, a romantic event. What are your favourite smells? What memory goes with them?

......................................................................

......................................................................

......................................................................

......................................................................

......................................................................

......................................................................

......................................................................

......................................................................

......................................................................

......................................................................

......................................................................

......................................................................

......................................................................

......................................................................

......................................................................

......................................................................

......................................................................

......................................................................

......................................................................

......................................................................

......................................................................

......................................................................

......................................................................

**36** Bring your awareness to your nose. What can you smell right here, right now. What comes in first? Second? Close one nostril and try again. Then alternate. Does it make a difference?

**37** Purposefully seek out a scent that you love: a favourite perfume, a fresh flower, clean linen, newly mown grass or a festive spice.

*Fill this bubble with adjectives that bubble up in your mind as you smell it.*

**38** Walk to your bookshelf and take down the first book that your hand touches. Open it to a random page and read a few lines.

*Write them down here.*

**39** Move your mind with games that keep your thoughts agile. When reading a newspaper, mentally rearrange a sentence to put the words in alphabetical order. Think back to your primary school friends – can you remember their surnames? What was the phone number of the first home you lived in? Name your first pet.

*Jot down the things you remember here, and list any you don't . . . they may come back to you another day.*

DAILY NEWS

PUZZLES

40 Even the most familiar walk will throw up surprises. You may realise this when you cross a local street at a different point and suddenly notice something new. Sketch the street on which you live or work. Do it from memory, fleshing out names of shops, street signs, trees and landmarks. Later, walk down the street to see how accurate your recollection was. Add in the things you missed.

**41** For something that is above your head, all day every day, you probably pay the sky very little attention. Yet, ironically, if you did look up, you'd gain access to the most beautiful slice of perspective. Spend some time now, sketching the sky exactly as it appears above you.

**42** When you breathe in you activate your sympathetic nervous system. When you breathe out you activate your parasympathetic nervous system. The latter stimulates the vagus nerve, which soothes and relaxes you. So, the next time you feel stressed, focus on making your exhale longer than your inhale. The ideal balance is two-to-one.

*Try it. With each exhalation, say the words in your mind:*

**'THIS IS ME BREATHING'**

**43** Think of the heartache you might save yourself if you just pause for a moment before speaking. Take time to rewrite the script of a conversation you'd like to have again. Then, make peace with what was, and what is, and let it go.

**44** What enjoyable activities have you not tried since childhood? Skipping? Using a Hula Hoop? Playing hopscotch? Set an intention to revisit one childhood activity a month. That's reclaiming joy in action!

# 45

Polish up your colour vocab. It's so satisfying to be able to describe shades and hues in greater depth, adding subtler brushstrokes to our everyday lives. Pick out something in plain sight, that is 'blue'. Now consider, is it aqua, royal, cerulean, azure? Not sure? Use the colour charts that follow to hone your hue ID skills, and have fun making up names for the missing ones.

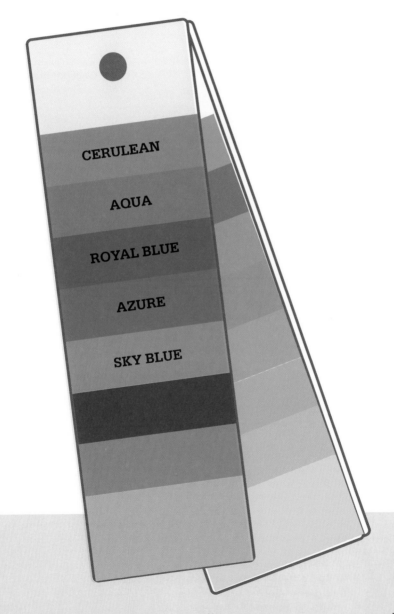

CERULEAN

AQUA

ROYAL BLUE

AZURE

SKY BLUE

**46** For many of us, our working space is also the space in which we spend the most time. Ensure yours is conducive to joy: take the time to select flowers or plants, place pictures or artwork, scent with candles or a diffuser. Once you've invited joy into the space, how does the way you approach work change?

**47** A jug of water can be an opportunity for joy. Source a pleasing second-hand vessel and, after a good clean, fill it with filtered water, fresh herbs, berries or slices of lime or lemon. Sip away while you work. Transform a daily 'must' into a welcome pleasure.

**48** If stress is building up and you find yourself without an opportunity to vent, reach for your 'valley' point. Place your hand flat on a surface, palm down. Find the acupressure point at the base of the 'V' in the firm piece of skin between the thumb and first finger. Press firmly for up to a minute to activate the body's natural de-stressing action.

**49** Close your eyes.
**COUNT TO TEN**.
Reopen them. What's
the first thing your
eyes are drawn to.

*Draw it here.*

**50** Mind games can be fun. While waiting or whiling away some time alone, challenge yourself. Pick a category – films/authors/capital cities – and move from A to Z, in your mind. For an extra challenge, try to come up with choices that begin and end with a given letter – for example, Oslo.

**51** If someone acts unfairly, challenge yourself to see that person through an empathetic lens. If their behaviour seems irrational, put yourself in their shoes – what might have made you do the same thing?

**52** Twenty-eight bones, thirty joints and more than one hundred muscles, tendons and ligaments – that's your feet: biological marvels. But how often do you treat them as such? Squeezed into shoes, hidden beneath socks – it's time to resurrect your soles! The simple act of redistributing your weight can help: fifty per cent on each foot, with fifty per cent between the ball and heel of each foot. If you catch yourself off-kilter, re-align. Keep doing so, until you begin to feel that sense of natural balance.

**53** Decorate this beautiful meadow with flowers, grasses and wildlife to wander through and get lost within.

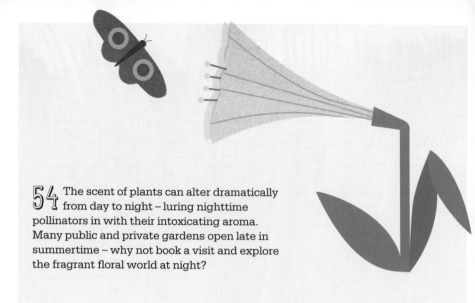

**54** The scent of plants can alter dramatically from day to night – luring nighttime pollinators in with their intoxicating aroma. Many public and private gardens open late in summertime – why not book a visit and explore the fragrant floral world at night?

**55** Every walker has a unique gait and rhythm. If waiting at a bus stop or train station, or wandering down the street yourself, tune into the patter and tap of others' footsteps. What's their tempo?

*Tap them out here with dots for short steps, and dashes for the longer ones.*

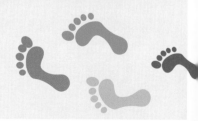

**56** Make a toe-tapping playlist of the songs you simply cannot sit still to. Listen to it when everyone else around you is still and stoney-faced (on a commuter train or in a traffic jam, perhaps). Imagine everyone bursting into a crescendo of song and dance. Smiles all round.

**57** Remind yourself regularly of mantras and sayings that inspire and uplift you. Add them at intervals to your phone's calendar. Each time one pops up with a happy alert, it'll be like receiving mail from a great friend.

*Make a list of your favourites here to get you started.*

**58** Open your wardrobe and pull out the first item of clothing your heart is drawn to. Wear it today!

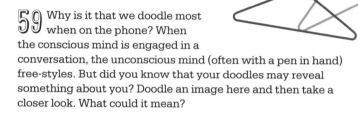

**59** Why is it that we doodle most when on the phone? When the conscious mind is engaged in a conversation, the unconscious mind (often with a pen in hand) free-styles. But did you know that your doodles may reveal something about you? Doodle an image here and then take a closer look. What could it mean?

**60** Have fun drawing the opposite sides of these everyday objects. They have been cut in half along a line of symmetry, but you can make them as reflective and realistic, or as abstract and outrageous, as you like.

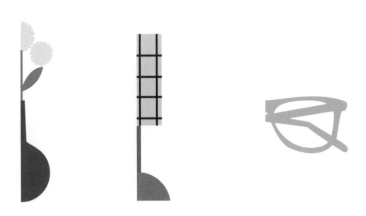

**61** The meditative action of whittling wood has been proven to lower stress levels, slow breathing and boost joy.

*Draw, and then cut, a spoon from this piece of wood. What shape, colour and size will you choose?*

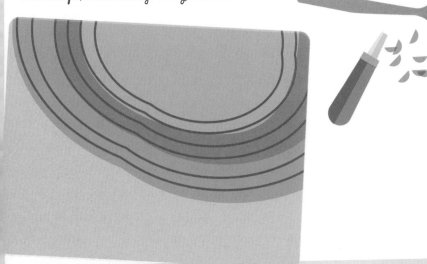

# UNWIND TIME

Long before the age of technology, nighttime was known only as the land of nod: once the sun set and the sky fell dark, all work and activity necessarily ceased, and the more restful part of the day began. Today, with endless sources of artificial light and their accompanying stimulation, we have moved further and further away from our natural body clocks and circadian rhythms. As a result, many of us struggle to sleep well, and yet we are wired to do just that – to rise with vim and gusto, and

slumber with ease and depth. It's time
to start slowly moving our body clocks a
little closer to their natural rhythms, taking
our lead from the natural world around
us, generous in its hints and clues as to
how, when and why we should prepare
ourselves for sleep. And indeed, when we
choose to 'prepare' for sleep, we accept
that sleep often requires a little laying
of the groundwork – from the repetition
of easeful melodies to the lulling calm of
mantras, soothing teas and somniferous
scents. There is also a need to reflect back
on the day that has passed – to collect the
treasures and store them away for another
time, knowing that once down on paper,
they need no longer be carried around in
the mind. When we approach our nights
as we approach our days – with clear,
quiet intention – things unfold just as they
should . . . just as nature intends.

**62** Once upon a time, we would have lain to sleep with the sunset and risen with the sunrise. To regulate our sleep patterns today, in this 'always on' world, the best thing we can do is stick to a regular rising and sleeping time. What are the ideal times for you to get into bed, to fall asleep, to wake up and to begin your day?

*Sketch your intentions on the clock.*

**63** Mark the bridge between work and home with a scent. Before stepping over the threshold of your home – particularly if the day has been long and trying – slow down, breathe deep and reach into your coat pocket. Keep something fragrant there – cardamom pods, for example. Take a couple, crush them, breathe the earthy aroma and feel ready to step inside.

*Doodle the contents of your fragrant pocket here.*
*Choose something new to pop into it tomorrow.*

**64** Many flowers curl their petals up at dusk and unfurl them at dawn. Evening primroses and moonflowers (a night blooming variety of the morning-glory) are so called because they bloom at night.

*Add magical petals to these flowers, ready to attract their night-flying pollinators.*

**65** Blue light from electronic devices has been shown to interfere with the body's melatonin production – and we need melatonin to begin our sleep-inducing cycle. Get out your diary – on which nights of the week can you realistically commit to a screen curfew, ideally two hours before bedtime?

**66** Did you know that dolphins can switch off half their brains and close one eye, allowing them to be half asleep and half awake at the same time? Or that giraffes sleep standing up for roughly thirty minutes a day, with one eye open and their ears twitching?

**67** Yoga nidra, or yogic sleep, is one of the most restorative practices available to us. The simple process of lying down, warm and comfortable, while following a gentle, guided meditation, beautifully unfurls the body and mind. Find one you like from the countless meditation apps and free downloads available.

**68** It's time to make your bed. Have fun sketching beautiful patterns, colours and cosy touches on this welcoming bed . . . then imagine climbing into it and drifting off into a deep sleep.

**69** 'Lulla' and 'bye' – these two words were combined in the 1500s to make the 'lullaby' that we now sing to our children. But lullabies soothe the singer, too. Pen some simple words of your own to bring calm to the end of your day, and set them to your favourite gentle tune.

*Write your lullaby here.*

**70** Think about the things that soothe you the most. A mug of cocoa? The smell of lavender? A loving cuddle? Come up with **ten things** and have fun inviting them into your nighttime wind-down routine. Aim to enjoy at least one every evening.

*Write your list of ten here.*

..................................................
..................................................
..................................................
..................................................
..................................................
..................................................
..................................................
..................................................
..................................................
..................................................
..................................................
..................................................
..................................................
..................................................
..................................................
..................................................
..................................................
..................................................
..................................................
..................................................

**71** 'Legs up the wall' is, officially, the most relaxing yoga pose of all.

*Colour in these lovely legs, before going off to enjoy some limbo-limb time yourself.*

**72** These foods are proven to help us feel sleepy.

*Colour them in as reminders of good snooze food.*

**73** Though green tea contains caffeine, it also contains L-theanine, which has been shown to promote relaxation, by raising GABA, serotonin and dopamine levels. It also enhances alpha brain waves – the type associated with relaxation. Anyone sensitive to caffeine should not have more than one cup a day.

**74** Enjoy personalising your favourite mug, here, before choosing some sleepy tea suggestions from the list below.

**75** These naturally sleep-inducing flowers make for an ideal bedtime tea.

*Bring their beauty to life with colour.*

PASSIONFLOWER

CHAMOMILE

LIME FLOWER

OAT FLOWER

**76** Rubbing your eyes when tired stimulates the lacrimal gland, which lubricates and soothes the eyes. It also stimulates the muscles that move the eye and this reflex in turn slows the heart, which, some studies suggest, leads to a feeling of relaxation.

*Use relaxing swirls to fill in these eyes . . . the repetitive circle has been found to be one of the most soothing to look at. Some say it is even . . . hypnotic . . .*

**77** Two of the most powerful mantras you can repeat to yourself at bedtime are...

'I GIVE MYSELF PERMISSION TO REST'

and

'NOTHING IS NEEDED OF ME RIGHT NOW'

Try these when you are struggling to relax.

*Add a third mantra of your own to the mix, one that really resonates with you.*

UNWIND TIME

# 78

Writing down your thoughts and feelings at the end of each day is a wonderful way to clear the mind, and clean the slate ahead of sleep. Use these pages to jot down the very first words that rise up into your mind the moment you put your pen to the paper. Don't judge the words that rise up – simply let them flow out. Once written, release them from your mind.

**79** Write down **five** recent, joyful memories to treasure. Add them to this treasure chest. Keep coming back every few days to add more.

1.

2.

3.

4.

5.

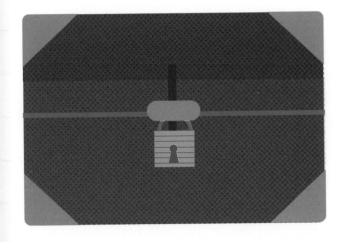

# 80

List one thing that you will do tomorrow, to promote joy in another.

..................................................................................................................

..................................................................................................................

..................................................................................................................

..................................................................................................................

..................................................................................................................

..................................................................................................................

..................................................................................................................

# 81

Twilight is that most magical time of day when the sun has just slipped below the horizon, bringing an ethereal glow to the earth. Set an intention to sit and watch the sunset, then twilight.

*Sketch the scene here as an ode to nature's majesty and mystery.*

**82** Look up the times of the sunset for the next week. Make a gentle commitment to yourself to down tools at sunset if you can, and have an offline evening, with no screens at all.

*Jot the times down here.*

MONDAY ........................................................

TUESDAY .......................................................

WEDNESDAY ....................................................

THURSDAY .....................................................

FRIDAY ........................................................

SATURDAY .....................................................

SUNDAY ........................................................

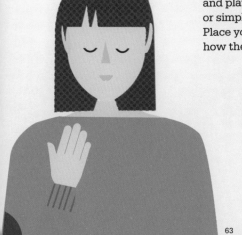

**83** Some sounds are naturally relaxing. The bija, or 'seed', mantras are primal sounds that are said to resonate with us, connecting us to our body's energy centres, or chakras. They include sounds such as OM (pronounced 'ohm') and LAM. Find a comfortable spot and play around with simple sounds, or simply hum with your mouth closed. Place your hand on your chest, and feel how the sound vibrates through it.

UNWIND TIME

*finish the story.*

## Once upon a time...

85 Can you remember a favourite bedtime story from childhood? What was it called? What characters were in it? Any lines you recall? Jot them down here, in your own storybook, as a reminder of nighttime's peaceful promise and potential.

**86** Name one enjoyable thing that you had hoped to do today, but did not find the time for. Realistically how long would it have taken? Plan this exact amount of time into your diary for the coming week, and do it.

*Make a note of your intention here.*

**87** At the end of the day your mind may feel a little like the active windows on your desktop computer – left with a hundred tabs open. Imagine that you have the ability to bookmark, save and then shut down those tabs.

*List the four most pressing thoughts you have on these tabs, one by one. Once you've finished, say out loud: I am now shutting down.*

**88** One of the most common places for us to hold tension is in the jaw. Try some facial yoga to loosen up the mandible. Simply open up your mouth as wide as it will go and then close your mouth again, before pretending to blow out a candle. Do this **three-step sequence** twenty times each night before bed. It will leave your jaw comfortably slack and soft.

**89** Set aside two hours of screen-free time in your diary and create a self-care intention right here, for what you'll do instead.

**90** Sketch items on this bedside table with a view to having a restful and relaxing environment at bedtime. If you can, bring the scene to life tomorrow, placing real objects in a way that mirrors your drawing.

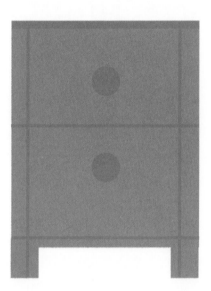

**91** Relax using a simple reclining yoga twist. Lying on your back on the floor, draw both knees in to your chest. Open your arms to the sides, like wings, and let your knees fall gently to one side. Move your head slowly from one side to the other. How does it feel when your head faces the same direction as your knees? And facing the opposite direction? Repeat, with your knees falling to the opposite side, and compare how it feels.

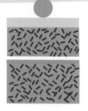

# THINK PRETTY THOUGHTS

**IT'S BETTER TO BE YOURSELF
AND LIVE WITH KINDNESS**

Imagine taking a guided tour of your daily
life, led by someone who has the ability to
reveal the magical within the mundane.
Someone who, with a flourish of a wand,
could illuminate the things happening all
around you, that you have never noticed
before – like flicking a switch on to an
alternate reality. There are many people
who profess that mindfulness is just such
a power – slowing us down enough to
notice, absorb and enjoy the little things.

The older I get, the slower I seem to
go – I love being able to do things at a
leisurely, even lazy, pace. When there is
an entire room to be cleaned, or a stack
of post to sort, rather than race through
it at the speed of light I like to put on
some great music, open all the windows,
kick off my shoes and just go about it
slowly and steadily. And, all of a sudden,
the obligatory act becomes something
altogether different – something restful
and pleasurable. I still get through what
needs to be done, but my energy is not
drained in the same way. This is the
inspiration behind this jolly chapter – filled
with fun, creative and heartfelt prompts to
help you find magic in the mundane. Enjoy
spontaneous scribbles, mindful exercises
and creative prompts that help exercise
the mind's ability to see the silver linings
in even the dimmest day. When we allow
ourselves to open up, even a little, to the
joyful potential we all possess, life explodes
in a kaleidoscope of goodness. And so
much of this goodness – this process
to reclaiming our joy as our birthright
– begins with our ability to be kind to
ourselves and one another.

# 92

Each day of the week has its own unique 'flavour'. . . slow and steady or muddled and manic. Colour in your dream week here, using a different colour for each day. Let your imagination run wild and free, envisioning each day just as you would like it to be: full of technicolour wonder.

## MONDAY

## TUESDAY

## WEDNESDAY

## THURSDAY

## FRIDAY

## SATURDAY

## SUNDAY

**93** Instead of living by your to-do list, reclaim joy with a daily love list. For each day, list one new activity or experience to look forward to. It can be as simple as enjoying a slice of cake and cuppa in the garden, or taking the first step towards a bigger project, such as learning a new language, or trying a new craft.

*Write your seven-day love list here.*

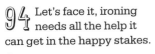

MONDAY

TUESDAY

WEDNESDAY

THURSDAY

FRIDAY

SATURDAY

SUNDAY

**94** Let's face it, ironing needs all the help it can get in the happy stakes.

*Have fun doodling your own short stack, here.*

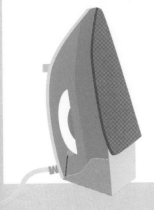

**95** We are, all of us, multitudes. A lovely way to ease the mind is to imagine yourself within a column of light, with the different parts of your personality circling you: grumpy, optimistic, honest, anxious, judgmental, playful.

*Create your own word circle, here, with you sitting in the middle. List all the words that occur to you as soon as they come to mind.*

**96** Having created your word circle, imagine that none of the words, or personalities, are any better than the others. None are good or bad. They just 'are'. Which words keep drawing you back? Which do you feel resistant to? Whatever you feel, avoid assigning value or meaning to it.

*Now colour in your circle, so that all of the parts' become one 'whole' and write your name in the middle.*

**97** The marvellous **Mary Poppins** sang about how important it is to find the fun in all that we do, however dull. There are a myriad of ways to make the mundane magical. Try singing operatic classics while vacuuming or add a couple of drops of mood-boosting essential oil to the sink while washing up (lemon is a great reviver).

**98** List your **five** least favourite chores below

1. ........................................................ ........................................................

2. ........................................................ ........................................................

3. ........................................................ ........................................................

4. ........................................................ ........................................................

5. ........................................................ ........................................................

**99** Add an idea beside each chore in your list to transform it from **dreaded to joyful**.

THINK PRETTY THOUGHTS

**100** Eating with full concentration can transform every bite – from the smell, colour and texture of the food, to the way its flavour alters depending on what part of the tongue it touches. Start small – try a berry or a chocolate button – and give it your full attention while you eat it. **Does it taste different?**

**101** **Quick:** how many teeth do you have? No idea? Isn't it funny that we can have a mouthful of them, but not even be aware how many there are? The next time you brush your teeth, take the time to count each one.

**102** Remember those triple-striped toothpastes? Have fun creating your own technicolour toothpaste here – what flavours would you combine?

**103** Let your mind wander back to a time when you thought all was lost. Now allow yourself to trace your steps to where you sit today. What moment changed your course for the better? What word or action or thought altered your beliefs in yourself at that time? Keep them all here in your treasure box, where you, and you alone, are the most wonderful treasure of all.

........................................................................................................................

........................................................................................................................

........................................................................................................................

........................................................................................................................

........................................................................................................................

........................................................................................................................

........................................................................................................................

........................................................................................................................

........................................................................................................................

**104** Silver linings abound all around, even on the darkest days. Consider something that has caused you pain or discomfort in the past year. Now, feel into what you may have learned from this challenge. Don't overthink it – simply write down whatever comes up for you. Read over your words. **How does that feel?**

........................................................................................................................

........................................................................................................................

........................................................................................................................

........................................................................................................................

........................................................................................................................

........................................................................................................................

........................................................................................................................

........................................................................................................................

........................................................................................................................

........................................................................................................................

**105** Look at yourself in the mirror. Do not look away. Every thought or feeling that comes up, keep looking. Look until you feel that you really see something you have not seen before. Now give yourself a big smile.

**106** Draw your wondrous reflection in this mirror or add a photo of yourself into this space if you prefer. What loving words and thoughts will you have each and every day?

*Write them down in thought bubbles.*

**107** What's the loveliest thing anyone has ever said to you? If you have already forgotten, it's time to begin writing them down.

*Save this space for the expressions of love and joy that people share with you. Read back on these whenever you need an emotional boost.*

**108** Write a love letter to yourself as though you are your own best friend. Thank yourself for all that you have done over the years – the laughter, the adventures, the learning curves and kindnesses. Pop your letter into the envelope, and send it back to yourself when you are ready to receive it.

**109** Do you remember the riotous fun you had as a kid, when tasked with devising a new invention? If you could invent one thing now, what would it be? From the unlimited-ice-cream machine to a rucksack-jetpack, **let your mind run free.**

*Doodle your ideas here.*

**110** The more we practise positive thinking, the more it sticks. What's your perpetual pet peeve? How can you reframe it? Is there a funny side? Use this perspective-o-meter to draw your peeve at the size it really is in comparison to the enormity of a life-or-death concern. Give your peeve another look . . . has it shrunk in importance?

**111** Saying something out loud can help shift the perspective of it. If you're upset about something, talk about it out loud to yourself right now. Listen to yourself as though you were listening to a best friend.

*Without labouring over it, write down the advice you'd give.*

**112** Be the reason someone smiles today. When you think a kind thought, don't keep it to yourself. Share it with the person who made you think it and watch that kindness multiply.

**113** With so much of our communication reliant on our devices, we've lost the joy of curling up with a stack of old letters and reminiscing.

*Find a favourite message on your phone and write it out here to keep forever.*

114 If you have family members or friends who knew you well as a child, give them a call and ask them to share the funniest memory they have of you as a kid. Remind yourself of this whenever life feels too serious.

115 Annotate these lovely kindness notes with 'pats on the back' for all you have to be proud of. Stick them where you'll see them each day – at your desk, on the bathroom mirror, in your purse.

**116** One of the main things that drains our energy is trying to do too many things at once. Give yourself permission to do just one thing at a time for one entire day. Think about the order you'll do things in, and – most importantly – plan in plentiful time to rest, too – as a priority, not an afterthought.

**117** Did you know that even if your smile is fake, your brain registers it as a positive response and that can lift the mood? Choose a day to set yourself reminders to smile more (even when you may not feel like it). You may be surprised at how much better you feel at the day's end.

**118** Every smile is different – a unique miracle.

*Have fun adding smiles to these cheery characters.*

**119** Some people beam kindness and happiness from their faces. Have you met someone like that? What do you imagine them thinking, that makes them so?

*Fill this head with happy thoughts.*

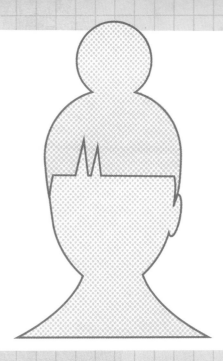

**120** Psychologists have found that we need five compliments to mitigate the negative effect on our psyches of one criticism. Have fun erasing the residue of past criticism with a whole beautiful barrage of compliments.

**121** Find two photographs of yourself, one in which you are completely relaxed and at home in your body, being kind to and accepting of yourself, and the other where you are self-conscious and lacking in confidence. Look closely into the eyes of the you who felt both things. What comes up?

THINK PRETTY THOUGHTS

# NATURE'S PLAYGROUND

**THERE IS SO MUCH JOY TO BE HAD FOR FREE, ALL AROUND US IN NATURE**

Remember those minibeast hunts from childhood, spending entire afternoons on our tummies, trailing an army of ants; picking petals for natural 'perfume'; climbing trees and building dens? It's in nature that we often feel most at ease, and the resurgence of nature-based trends, such as forest bathing, wild swimming and cabin living, all point to a collective move back to the earth; a need to strip away the excessive and the unnecessary, and get blissfully back to basics. And you don't need to seek out storybook meadows or idyllic coastlines to reap the rewards; wherever you live, nature will find a way of poking its nose into your business, and it's your duty to welcome it with open arms. In this chapter, we remind ourselves of what nature has to offer us, not only as the ultimate, limitless adventure playground, but as an abundant source of natural influences in our everyday lives: from happy-making houseplants to mood-boosting moonbeams and brilliant bird calls to sky-gazing scribbles. And, in keeping with our hand-on-heart motto in this one precious life – our pledge always to give back – wherever you live, the ethics of the countryside code serve us all well: 'Tread lightly. Leave no trace. Do no harm.' Amen to that.

**122** Numerous studies into the wellbeing of hospital patients have found that those with a window overlooking trees recover more quickly. But you don't have to be ill to fill your room with a view.

*Decorate this plain pane with all the things you'd like to see growing outside your window.*

**123** The next time you're in a green space, take the time to sketch the plants you see, annotating how they move in the wind. Some ripple, others shake; some sway, others flap. **Nature's very own ballet.**

124 Pick a favourite outdoor spot and zoom in on one tiny patch of it early in the morning. Observe the flowers and insects, sounds and smells. Revisit the same spot at sunset. How is it different? What has changed the most? What remains the same?

125 There are as many distinct bird calls as there are human voices. The next time you're woken by a dawn chorus, see if you can pick out these distinctive tweets. The great tit makes a clear and repetitive call that sounds like 'tea-cher' 'tea-cher'. Spot the wren with its loud burst of song and extended rattle – like a machine gun – at the end of each call. The chiffchaff is an easy listen, repeating its own name, with a singsong 'chiff-chaff, chiff-chaff'.

126 Did you know that the moon does not produce any light? When we say 'moonlight' we refer only to the sun's light reflecting from the moon's rocky surface. Many ancient cultures lauded moonlight as a calming influence. In Ayurveda, cooling moonbathing was prescribed to those who were too hot-blooded.

*Etch your own slice of silvery, serene moon here. Don't forget the man (or woman) in the moon, too.*

**127** Earthing isn't an alien concept. When we stand barefoot on the ground, the soles of our feet absorb Earth's faint electromagnetic frequencies. This deeply de-stressing exchange is simple and free – all you need to do is take off your shoes.

**128** Just as we used to look up at the clouds as kids, imagining dragons and steam trains, the Japanese art of hirameki gives the imagination a welcome field day. It involves doodling what you see onto a series of ink blots (which look a lot like puffs of cloud). Hirameki even means 'flash of inspiration'.

*Have fun letting your imagination run free, by embellishing these blue sky and cloud ink blots.*

**129** Ever suckled honey from the honeysuckle? Children are often drawn to the sweet scent of this creamy-white flower. When you pinch the end off the bloom, to remove the stamen, a small drop of honey-like nectar appears that is both edible and delicious.

**130** One of the simplest ways to attract more joy into your garden is to make it a thriving environment for birds and pollinators. These pollinator-attracting plants are favourites with bees, butterflies and beetles.

HONEYSUCKLE

BUDDLEIA

BLUEBELL

COMFREY

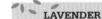
LAVENDER

CALENDULA

FOXGLOVE

**131** Etch a house into this majestic tree. Fill your imagination with the mischief you'll get up to, up and away in your own private arboreal abode.

**132** When was the last time you swam in the sea? Numerous studies have shown that sea swimming reduces stress and insomnia, while also increasing longevity and holistic wellbeing. Mimic the benefits with a briny bath. Add two big cups of sea salt to the tub, sink in, and let your mind sail away.

**133** Embellish this Hokusai-style great wave, using meditative swirls and strokes. Brush pens or watercolours are ideal.

**134** Houseplants make us happy – innumerable studies support the link between a foliage-friendly home and improved wellbeing.

*Brighten up this room with some jubilant, jungle-inspired doodles.*

**135** You don't have to hike hills and climb mountains to experience the scenic route in life. Every now and then plan extra time into a dull daily journey and plot out a more picturesque course.

**136** If there is something you do every day that you can do irrespective of location, why not take it outside? The force of habit often leads us to stay indoors, or at a desk, when we can just as easily take our work/lunch/phone call/ meeting in a natural setting.

**137** When we are in nature, we often remain so consumed with our thoughts that we miss the tiny details. Nature journalling is a wonderful way to develop the art of really SEEING. The next time you head out, take your journal with you. Collect fallen leaves, flowers to press, bark to etch. Find the time to write an entry in your journal each time, too.

**138** What we hear when we are in nature is as intrinsic to the relaxing experience as what we see, smell and touch. Why not replicate this by creating a nature soundscape from the thousands of downloadable tracks available online? Choose all of your favourite sounds – birdsong, ocean, wind, rain – and have it playing in the background at home, or while you work.

**139** If you cannot easily get away from the digital world, imbue your screen time with influences from the natural world. Studies have shown that even looking at digital images of nature relaxes us.

*Create your own soothing screensaver here.*

**140** You might know an oak from a maple, but that's just the tip of the forest! Most European countries have around 250 species of tree, North America has around 1,000 and Australia has well over 4,000. Challenge yourself to identify one unfamiliar species each time you set off on a long nature walk.

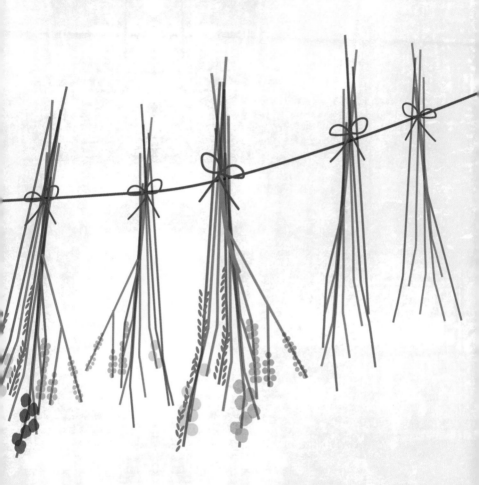

**141** Fresh flowers always brighten a room and dried flowers can be just as beautiful. If drying your own, simply tie the stems with string and hang the bunch upside down in a dry place that gets a good stream of air and light.

*Add drying blooms to these string-tied stalks, all in a pretty row.*

142 The natural world at night is quite a sight. Armed with a torch and a plan, choose one night each year to go on a nighttime safari. Many national nature-based organisations run guided nocturnal walks, so it's worth seeking them out. Be slow, stealthy and respectful, as you keep an excited eye out for badgers, hedgehogs and foxes.

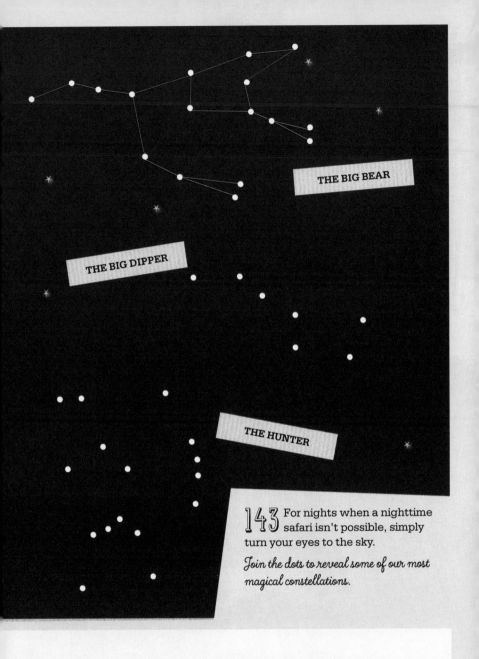

THE BIG BEAR

THE BIG DIPPER

THE HUNTER

**143** For nights when a nighttime safari isn't possible, simply turn your eyes to the sky.

*Join the dots to reveal some of our most magical constellations.*

**144** We've all played 'what three things would you take if stranded on a desert island'. What would your three things be if you found yourself alone in the wild wilderness? And, yes, it's only fair to have both a very sensible, and a totally irresponsible version.

# 145

Spend a month marking up your very own moon map. From new moon to full moon, jot down your thoughts and feelings each night, for twenty-eight days. You may want to photocopy these pages so you can carry on using them, month after month.

**NOTES:**

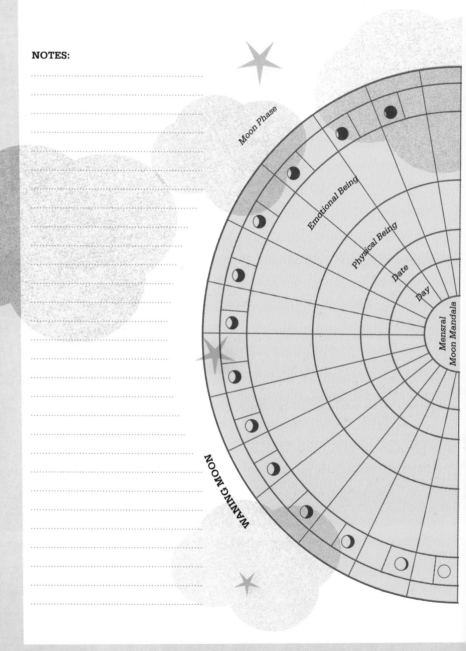

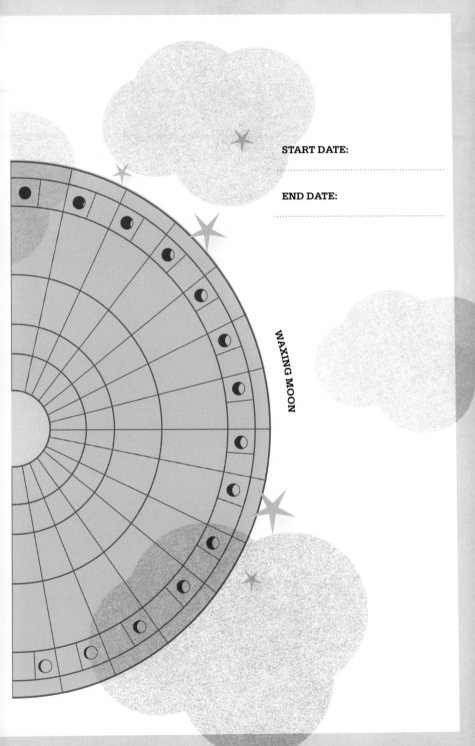

START DATE:

...............................

END DATE:

...............................

WAXING MOON

NATURE'S PLAYGROUND

**146** A lovely way to pay more attention to what is all around your feet when you are out walking in nature is to make a foraged crown. A joyful reminder of nature's generosity – a beautiful adornment, made from fallen treasure.

**147** These busy little ants are on a mission.

*Imagine their amazing story here.*

**148** Nature has inspired some of our very best poetry. Find one natural thing as your source of inspiration and write an 'ode' to it.

*Keep a note of your poem here.*

.................................................
.................................................
.................................................
.................................................
.................................................
.................................................
.................................................
.................................................
.................................................
.................................................
.................................................
.................................................
.................................................
.................................................
.................................................
.................................................
.................................................

**149** Freshly cut grass is one of the most popular smells of all. What natural things have aromas that you adore?

*Fill these bottles with them.*

**150** Man-made labyrinths have been found all over the world, some dating back more than four thousand years. Finger labyrinths are stones that have a labyrinth pattern carved or painted into them. Forage for big flat pebbles to make your own, or create one here. Then use it to trace your finger around slowly, imagining you are walking through the labyrinth. Whenever your thoughts wander, simply bring your mind back to the labyrinth.

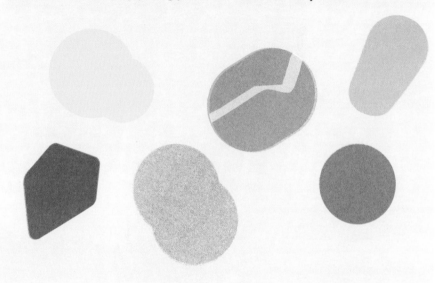

**151** You're never too old to make a daisy chain! Use a craft knife to pierce the thickest part of the stem, before threading another stem through it, until you have a full chain of daisies. Wear it as a crown or necklace, or drape it over a mirror or picture frame.

*Have fun embellishing this lovely flower chain, too.*

**152** A terrarium is a tiny garden housed inside a sealable glass container. There's no need to invest in a pricey planter – a big old jar works nicely!

*Fill this jar with soil, pebbles, greenery, flowers, butterflies – whatever takes your flight of fancy.*

**153** Time for some succulent love.

*Give this cute cactus the full colour treatment.*

# HOPEFUL LIVING

## RETHINK, REUSE AND REPURPOSE

When I think of sustainability the same image always pops into my head. It is my Turkish grandmother's fridge. It's fifty years old. It was an expensive purchase in its day – akin to buying a first car. But, there it is, fifty years later, still humming, cooling, ever reliable. Made to last, made for life. The ease with which we can now buy, replace and discard commodities – and our ever-growing convenience culture, rife with disposables that were not made to biodegrade – has had a devastating effect on the Earth. Perhaps we all got too busy to darn our socks and mend our shoes, or perhaps the items in question are so cheap to buy and so easy to obtain that we could replace them ten times over in the time it takes to complete the repair. We consume so insatiably that should we continue like this, many scientists posit that Earth's resources will be exhausted before the century is out. There is nothing joyful about this. But there is something so powerfully hopeful about repurposing another's waste, about making a new, beautiful, useful thing from rubbish. That feels like a reclaim joy revolution! Here, then, we celebrate the many inspiring and practical ways to breathe new life into things that would ordinarily end up in the bin. It's time to rethink, reuse and repurpose in order to transform what comes into and goes out of our homes.

**154** Six million tonnes of coffee grounds are sent to landfill every year. That's madness when you consider how useful they can be. Mix with oil to make a great skin scrub; sprinkle into the soil of acid-loving plants, such as carrots and radishes; place them in a bowl in the fridge to absorb any odours.

*Challenge yourself to come up with as many ideas as you can and add them to this coffee cup, here.*

**155** Plastic bottles of all sizes make great storage. You may not want to use them for food, but why not use them as sorters for buttons, screws, tacks, pins and other bits and bobs? A tidy shelf, lined with sorted bottles, is a satisfying nod to joy, reclaimed!

# 156

Today, it's easier than ever to do your bit for the environment. Why not start at home? Most household cleaning jobs need only one of three inexpensive things – vinegar, sodium bicarbonate, or soap (pure liquid Castile soap is a great natural option).

*Fill these bottles-for-life with your chosen cleaning combos and then make them for yourself.*

## WHAT DOES WHAT?

**Vinegar:** Descales; great for making glass shine mixed 50/50 with water.

**Vinegar + sodium bicarbonate:** Great for unblocking pipes, cleaning ovens, scouring sinks and floors.

**Sodium bicarbonate:** Absorbs odour; great in an open jar in the fridge or sprinkled over a carpet before vacuuming.

**Vinegar + Castile soap:** An amazing all-natural, all-purpose cleaning solution.

# 157

Make your bottle-for-life combinations more fragrant with a few drops of essential oil. The following are also naturally antibacterial: lemon, tea tree, sage, rosemary, eucalyptus, cedarwood and peppermint.

*Have fun adding details to the labels, to match your chosen essential oils.*

**158** Visible mending repairs damage to textiles with flourish and flare – stitching that begs to be shown off! Countless online tutorials explore many different types of stitch and technique. Start here, by creating your very own 'patch' designs.

**159** Did you ever make paper dolls as a child? Take photographs of items of clothing you haven't worn for a while. Print them and cut them out, or sketch them directly onto this dress-up-dolly, as a reminder of the great outfits hiding away in your wardrobe.

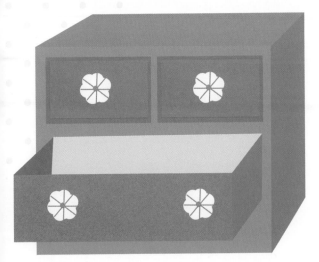

**160** Open any drawer in your house. Take everything out. Count the number of items. In the drawer oposite draw only the things you really need, then place these real items back in the drawer.

**161** Draw the unneeded items from the previous exercise in the space below. For each one, challenge yourself to come up with a new way to use it. If there isn't one, look to find someone who needs it – from a local charity to a community swap-shop or second-hand goods website.

**162** Many of us are now saying no to single-use plastic. But, inevitably, we all have some old plastic bottles and bags hanging around at home. Resist the urge to throw them away and find a new use for them instead. Read on in this chapter for ideas.

*Use these ten green bottles to note down ideas you want to try, and decorate them, too. Refer back to these pages whenever you have a plastic bottle that needs a new lease of life.*

**163** Make a bird feeder from an old bottle. Cut a small window in the side of the bottle so that the birds can land on it to feed. Don't make it so large that seeds pour out. Make some small holes in the bottom of the bottle so that any rainwater can drain. Hang the feeder from a branch using a piece of wire or string secured around the fastened bottle cap.

*Add bright and beautiful birds to this recycled feeder.*

**164** There are thousands of amazing repurposing tutorials on the internet, so get creative. For example, character-themed plant pots require little more than a pair of scissors, acrylic paint and marker pens – let loose your imagination!

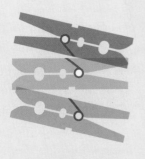

**165** The average person owns twice as many things as someone who lived fifty years ago. Back then, many people had to rely on resourcefulness and ingenuity to make do with what they had rather than finding cheap, quick-fix solutions.

*Have fun giving each of these everyday objects a new lease of life. While you work, think about how many different ways each can be used.*

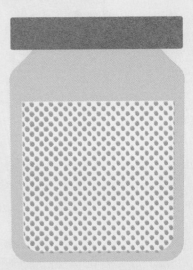

**166** Take a peek inside your recycling bin. What items are most commonly found there? Think about which of them you can source in a different, waste-free way, to keep the bin as empty as possible next time.

*Fill this imaginary bin with those common items.*

**167** Let's take a look inside the wardrobe. Count the number of clothes you have in there. Now, write down the number of clothes you have worn in the past six months. And the number you have not. If you own clothes you love, but never seem to wear, move them to the front of your wardrobe and look forward to wearing them this week.

**168** Set aside a morning to line up all the clothing and accessories that you love, but that are in need of repair. Save up the money you need to take them to a good tailor, seamstress or cobbler, and have them renewed for life.

*Each time you have something repaired, add it to this orderly wardrobe.*

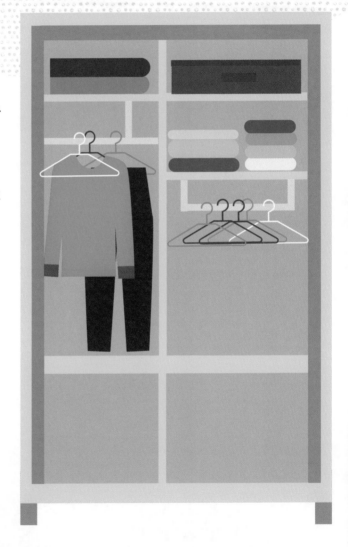

**169** Move from room to room letting your eyes fall on things you are not wholly fond of. If it doesn't **'spark joy'** (a term coined by minimalist Marie Kondo), set it aside.

**170** Take a photograph of an item in your house that no longer 'sparks joy' and send it to someone you think might like to offer it a new home. Or, upload the picture to a community sales platform, and see if it sparks joy for someone else.

*Fill this trunk with items in your home that no longer spark joy. Annotate the labels with names of people who might enjoy them instead.*

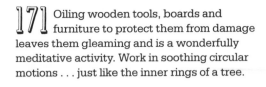

**171** Oiling wooden tools, boards and furniture to protect them from damage leaves them gleaming and is a wonderfully meditative activity. Work in soothing circular motions . . . just like the inner rings of a tree.

**172** Think about your most disposable household items, and how you can replace them with something of beauty, personal value and meaning, with a view to reclaiming joy in the process. For example, make bright, beautiful and reusable cleansing cloths from scraps of pretty fabric or resurrect the handkerchief to replace facial tissues. Embroider your name or a cheery picture in the corner.

**173** Fast fashion has created a world in which items of clothing are as cheap as they are throwaway, and the environmental impact is enormous. We rarely save up for something that we really want. What single item of clothing do you really need or want that you would be willing to save up for? Treat yourself to it only when you can afford it. How does it feel?

*Sketch the item of clothing here.*

**174** Set yourself a goal of refusing to buy any new clothing for a month. Then another . . . and keep going. If you need to replace something, consider seeking out a second-hand alternative first. After all, there's joy-a-plenty waiting to be reclaimed in thrift stores and charity shops.

**175** If you could learn one new skill to help you make and mend more effectively at home, what would it be?

*Write it down here, along with the first step you'll take today.*

**176** Blackberries, wild garlic and strawberries are just some of the foods that are commonly sold in plastic, but that can be foraged for free.

*Fill this trug with delicious foraged finds.*

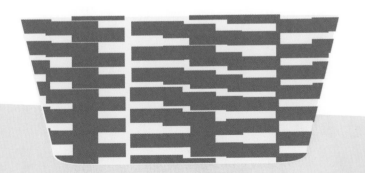

**177** The best advice regarding mindful consumerism is to wait a full week before buying something you want. If the 'want' dulls in that time, it is not worth it.

*Use this shopper to store scribbles of the few things you currently want, but won't buy until at least a week has passed.*

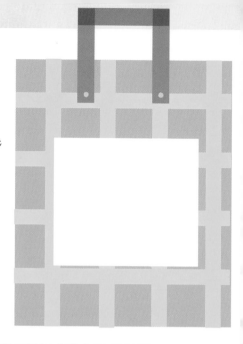

**178** Most unloved items simply need a good clean for a new lease of life – think of the vibrant light that floods in when you clean your windows.

*Imagine what's on the other side of these just-washed window panes. Paint the scene.*

**179** Unmendable and faded textiles have myriad uses. If you've a pile of clothes that are too shabby to sell or donate, cut them up to use as cleaning cloths and surface wipes, saving the less shabby parts for craft projects.

*Have fun filling in a patchwork quilt design here, taking inspiration from the fabrics in your own home.*

**180** Sturdy shoeboxes make for perfect storage containers. Cover them in old wrapping paper or pretty pages from magazines. Trace the shapes below to make your own custom labels.

**181** The next time you consider gifting a new toy to a child, consider the crazy statistic that the average child in the UK owns 238 toys, but only plays with 12 daily. What about you? Can you remember your favourite toys from childhood? What were they called?

**182** Studies have shown that we gain almost as much joy from window shopping and browsing as we do from physically purchasing things. If you're consumed by the consumer itch, try doing this for a week. You may be surprised to find that your urges are curbed.

**183** Let's practise a little of the Japanese art of kintsugi, when broken pottery is mended using golden joinery.

*Give these broken ceramics the kiss of life with golden-yellow seams.*

# THE HEARTFUL HOME

**IT'S TIME TO PLAY HOUSE –
FILL IT WITH JOY**

Home means something to us all
– something that does not rest solely upon
the bricks and mortar structures where
we find shelter and warmth. Home is a
place to be ourselves, a place to invite
and create joy, to let our hair down,
to cosy up with our loved ones or find
sweetest solace and silence in our own
good company. A heartful home is filled
with happiness. Even the smallest spaces

exude comfort and joy, not because they
are immaculate and elegant, but because
they are reflections of our personalities,
interests and beliefs. No two homes are
identical, just as no two people are exactly
alike. These physical expressions of our
selves house our memories, our creative
endeavours, our restful potential. And so
it feels crucial to the journey of reclaiming
joy, that they are not cluttered or
burdensome, but freeing and restorative.
This chapter starts with a space survey
to identify which areas may need your
attention. Then come ways in which you
can work to invite in the light, the loving,
the happy and the cosy hygge (there is,
after all, always room for a soft blanket,
flickering candle, happy houseplant).
Size is immaterial here. Even the tiniest
homes can be sanctuaries – inspiring and
beautiful – when filled with only those
things that nourish our potential for joy,
gratitude and wellbeing. Home is where
the heart is . . . when we let the heart
lead us where it will.

THE HEARTFUL HOME

**184** The dynamics of our daily spaces have a huge impact on our sense of wellbeing. Too much clutter, not enough light, doors that don't fully open, lack of fresh air or greenery – all will impede your ability to create joy. **Read on to take a space survey.**

**185** Which room do you spend the most time in? On a **scale of 1 to 5**, think about how you feel in the space: 1 is least joyful, 5 is most.

**186** Let your heart guide you around the room. What areas feel problematic, dingy, unloved?

*Note them down here.*

**187** Look around you: does your space need an update? Does clutter need to be cleared? Does more light need to be invited in? Do you need a bit more greenery? A lick of paint? Use this simple room plan to sketch out a solution.

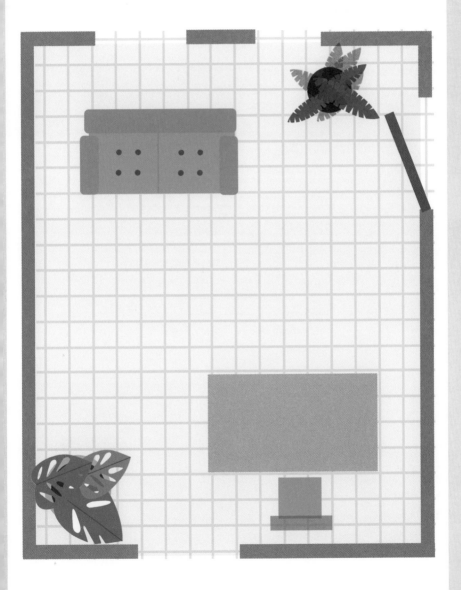

**188** Transform the humble tub into a place of peace and joy. Add flower petals, scented oil, salt, herbs, clays and even crystals to the water to elevate an everyday soak into a restorative ritual.

*Have fun transforming this bathtub, following the nudges of your own needs.*

**JOYFUL BATH INSPIRATION:**

Rose petals + magnesium salt = deeply relaxing

Oats + calendula = skin-soothing

Rosemary + Epsom salts = invigorating

**189** People across many cultures, use fire as a symbol of new beginnings.

*Write down three things you no longer want to carry into the next cycle of your life on paper scraps and throw them into a real fire.*

1. ........................................

2. ........................................

3. ........................................

190 A crystal is a natural miracle, a special kind of solid material in which the atoms fit together in a highly ordered repeating pattern. Each crystal is made up of different minerals and, therefore, different atoms, which, dependent on their weight and size, vibrate at different frequencies. This is what gives each crystal its unique properties. Here are five crystals associated with joy and happiness.

*Focus on thoughts that make you happy while you enjoy some mindful crystal colouring.*

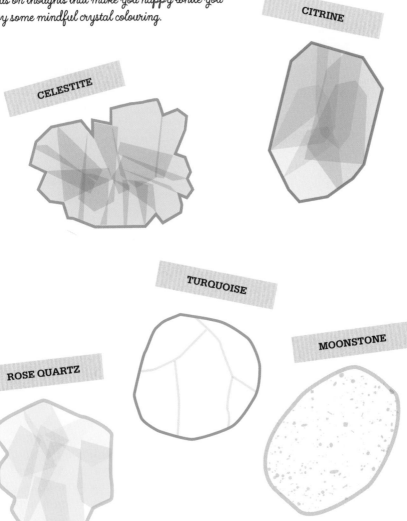

CITRINE

CELESTITE

TURQUOISE

MOONSTONE

ROSE QUARTZ

191 It's natural to feel in colour. A relaxing room may feel 'greenish-blue', while a bright, sunny room feels 'orange'. Enjoy creating a colour code for the rooms in your home. Revisit it next season. Has it changed?

..............................................
..............................................
..............................................
..............................................
..............................................
..............................................
..............................................
..............................................
..............................................

192 Essential oils bring joy-boosting benefits to all manner of daily duties. Proven mood-lifters include rose, lemon, neroli, tangerine and basil. Why not add a drop or two of joyful essential oils to a piece of paper, let it dry, and then slide it into this book? Each time you open it, you'll have a scented smile awaiting you.

193 Trace a favourite phrase or word that makes you smile onto this steamed-up bathroom mirror.

**194** Add light to this candle. Imagine the flame flickering in a darkened room as you work – meditative mind power in action.

**195** Have fun adding your own personal flourishes to this cosy corner.

THE HEARTFUL HOME

**196** Do you have a pet? What about an imaginary one? Bring this furry friend to life with colour and imagine giving him or her a gentle stroke while you work. *Purr.*

**197** The trend for tiny homes shows that more people are valuing their quality of life over the size of their abodes . When space is so limited, you're forced to choose only what you need and love. Whenever you consider what to bring into your home, give it the 'tiny home treatment'. Ask: Do I need it? Do I love it? **A no, means no.**

**198** All homes are made lovelier and healthier with the addition of some well-chosen houseplants. These air-purifying plants are ideal for city living, being as hardy as they are hardworking.

*Perk them up with some colour.*

**199** Lavender makes a wonderful fragrant, sleep-supporting tea. Plant up a little pot and pluck a few flowers to steep in hot water to drink before bedtime. Come late summer, cut the flowering heads back to the base of each stem and dry the flowers in a sunny spot, spread over a tea towel. Jar the dried purple heads to keep you in plentiful sleepy tea until the following summer.

**200** Eminently enlivening, rosemary is a great head clearer. Keep a generous fresh sprig hanging from the showerhead in the bathroom, for instantaneous energy-boosting steam.

**201** Chilly homes benefit from extra draught excluders and a spare blanket or three draped over beds and sofas.

*Bring joy and hygge warmth to this spartan futon with plush textiles and woolly blankets.*

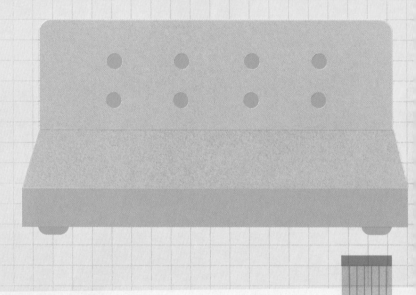

**202** Don't forget to keep your feet warm! In traditional Chinese medicine, the health of the heart is linked to the warmth of the feet. Enjoy a nightly warm foot spa: add herbs and salt to a large bowl, and fill with hot water. Afterwards, cosy your toesies up in your softest socks.

**203** When we keep special notes, letters and sketches in drawers or folders, we miss out on the joy of seeing them all the time. Invest in a beautiful large picture or poster frame, or elegant pinboard, and make a point of curating, displaying and enjoying your life's precious paper memories.

*Enjoy adding extras to this pretty pinboard, too.*

**204** Colour has a considerable impact on how we perceive a space. Paint these identical rooms in two very different colour palettes. **How do they look? How do they feel?**

**205** We often buy inexpensive art to fill a space on a wall, without thinking more deeply about what we want to feel when we look at it.

*Fill these frames with things that have a special meaning to you.*

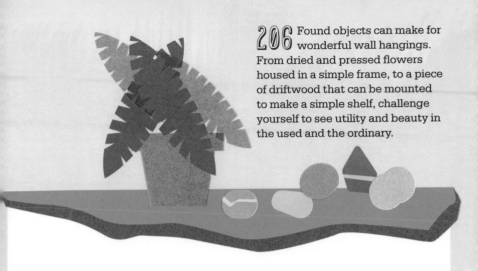

**206** Found objects can make for wonderful wall hangings. From dried and pressed flowers housed in a simple frame, to a piece of driftwood that can be mounted to make a simple shelf, challenge yourself to see utility and beauty in the used and the ordinary.

**207** Sliding into a freshly made bed is eminently joyful, and studies have shown that seventy-three per cent of us sleep better in clean sheets. Make a point of changing your sheets every week – both your senses and your sleep will thank you for it.

THE HEARTFUL HOME

# 208

The trailing woodsmoke from cottage chimneys is an evocative, wintry delight.

*Add wisps of whimsy to this rooftop scene.*

**209** Carry a little comfort around with you, even when far from home. From a small protective crystal to a favourite aromatherapy spray, sketch your home-comforts-to-go in this protective pouch.

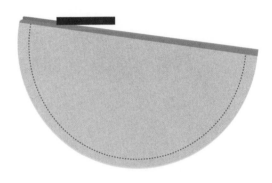

**210** Make a small pile of your favourite dog-eared books to reach for on rainy days. List their titles below as a reminder of best friends in bibliotherapeutic form.

..................................................................................

..................................................................................

..................................................................................

..................................................................................

..................................................................................

..................................................................................

..................................................................................

..................................................................................

**211** Every home has its own unique scent. You are aware of it the moment you walk in, be it wet dog or freshly baked bread. What would your 'uniquely you' home smell like?

**212** Every time you come home, greet your space as you would a fond, old friend. Come up with a greeting and enjoy saying it out loud (or thinking it, if you have company), to mark your joyful crossing over the threshold.

*Write your greeting here.*

**213** Walk through your front door. Is there something that immediately catches your eye and dampens your mood? Can it be moved / changed / fixed? If so, do it. If not, and it is not essential, it's time to say goodbye to it.

# 214

There is a front door on every street that stands apart from all the others.

*Give this front door a makeover that does just that.*

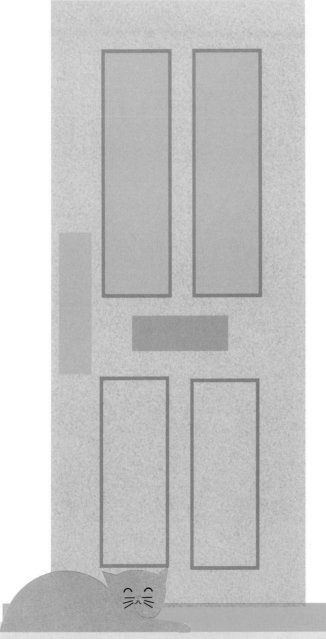

# HARVESTING HAPPINESS

**IT'S TIME TO LISTEN IN, SEASON BY SEASON**

As a wellbeing writer and editor of a mindfulness magazine, I frequently come across the same themes in my work, but none more so than the importance of seasonal, cyclical living. So much of modern life is driven not by our own innate needs and intelligent intuition, but by the relentless ticking of an arbitrary clock. There is an inherent disconnect here – we are not mechanized, programmable machines. Just as a flower is not made to bloom all year round, neither are we. And just as our calendar year has its fallow and fertile periods, so too should we. There is no joy in pushing against and forcing through; it's much better to rest, restore and reawaken, if only we can learn to listen a little more to our own needs, day by day and season by season. Here, then, we celebrate the cycles of nature – and how we can all adapt our busiest lives to a more conscious, seasonal rhythm. It all begins by paying a little more attention to the joy that abounds, for free, all around us, month by month. There is endless happiness to be found in the heart of Mother Nature – from gathering and foraging, to sowing and growing. You may or may not have a garden, but that is no barrier to dipping your toe into the seasonal soil with mindful ways to manage the space you do have, and prepare your pot, planter or little plot for the year ahead. Seasonal living is one of the most immediate and gratifying ways to bring joy into your home, to feel healthier and better supported and to save money in the process. From foolproof tips on what to grow when and how, to creative prompts to dust off those green fingers, pick up fresh ideas for ways to form a more beautiful and bountiful friendship with Mother Nature.

215 Seasonal living begins by thinking about the nature of each season – its qualities and attributes, colours and sounds. Use the following pages to flesh out the 'feeling' of each season, as it appears to you. Be as abstract or specific as you like.

WINTER

SPRING

SUMMER

AUTUMN

**216** Focus on the smell of each season. What aromas or scents really sing the season for you?

*Fill these four baskets with your vibrant favourites.*

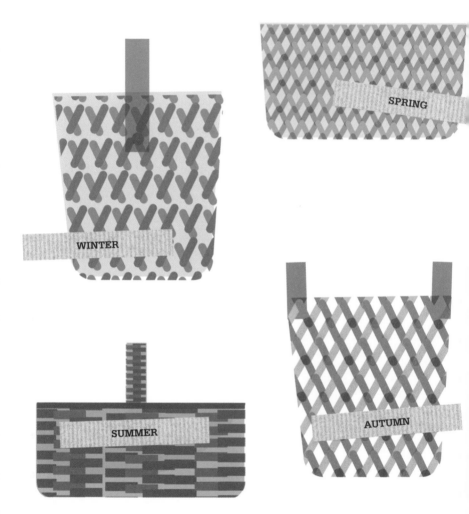

WINTER

SPRING

SUMMER

AUTUMN

**217** Thinking about the qualities and tastes of your favourite foods, consider how your cravings change through the year. This is nature's way of nourishing you – making you crave precisely what is most fresh and 'in season'. Spend a few minutes imagining the tastes of each season: fresh, crunchy and green in spring; water-rich, light and juicy in summer; sweet, earthy and warming in autumn; rich and hearty in winter.

**218** As more and more natural habitats are destroyed by deforestation and over farming, it becomes more important than ever to offer shelter in your own back garden. From late winter to earliest spring is when our feathered friends need a helping hand.

*Create your own funky bird box design here.*

**219** The silver birch tree is a symbol of spring in Celtic cultures, linked to the goddess Brigid, who brought about new beginnings.

*Etch your hopes into the bark of this silver birch.*

**220** The five easiest fruits and veggies to grow without a garden are **lettuce greens**, **carrots**, **tomatoes**, **chillies** and **spring onions**. Plant seeds in spring, for summer pickings, straight from pot to plate.

**221** What do you crave right now?
Add it to your shopping list.

**222** Foraging is not only great fun, but brilliantly frugal. Abundant in spring, broad-leafed wild garlic likes damp, shady woodland soil and is also found bordering fields and hedgerows. Easily identified by its unmistakable highly garlicky scent, it's a treat in pesto and pasta sauces.

**223** You can buy flower and tree identification guides cheaply in most second-hand bookshops. Set aside an early-summer's afternoon to play plant detective. Try to identify as many things that grow in your own garden or close to where you live as you can. What was your favourite?

*Draw it here.*

**224** If you lack outdoor space, why not make a mini garden within a big pot or planter? Simply fill it with good soil and compost and use it to plant micro plants and herbs. You can keep it by the front or back door, or even inside if you're not bothered about muddy crumbs.

*Enjoy filling this mini garden with green things, too.*

**225** Nature is a wonderful reminder of how much happens beneath the surface. Even when things look calm and in control, there is much in motion and action – you only notice the patterns and interrelationships when you look for long enough. Spend ten minutes looking at a small patch of grass in a natural environment.

*What do you notice?*

.......................................................................................................................

.......................................................................................................................

.......................................................................................................................

.......................................................................................................................

.......................................................................................................................

.......................................................................................................................

**226** Lashings and lashings of lemonade go down a treat on sweltering summer days. Simply mix the juice of a freshly squeezed lemon or lime (or half of each), into a big glassful of water, add a teaspoon of honey (sweeten to taste) and a handful of crushed, fresh mint.

**227** Nature is ingenious. Often we find that the benefits of a food mirror the food itself. Examples include kidney beans (yes, they actually benefit our kidneys); almonds, which aid eye health, and brain-like walnuts, which have been proven to support cognitive function.

HARVESTING HAPPINESS

**228** Studies have shown that children who grow up on farms, exposed to good, microbe-rich mud and dirt on a daily basis, are far less likely to have allergies. Sink your hands into soil. Feel it. Smell it. *Describe it.*

**229** At the summer solstice, the sun rises earliest and sets latest, giving us all a little more time in our day. What will you do with those precious extra minutes? **Make it special.**

**230** A ripe red tomato is one of summer's sweetest delights. If you have grown or bought more than you need, don't let a bite go to waste. Simply whiz up with a pinch of sea salt and some fresh basil or oregano, for perfect passata that can be frozen for up to six months.

**231** Have you ever spent time watching bees waggle dance from flower to flower? If you stay for long enough, you'll see more and more bees arrive to collect pollen and nectar as news of the source spreads. Spend a summer's afternoon watching the bees and follow the directions of their dancing hive mates.

**232** Wild strawberries are Mother Nature's secret gift. Hidden beneath verdant leaves with serrated edges, the vivid red fruits are far smaller than cultivated varieties. But boy, do they pack a flavour punch! It's rare to find them in shops, so make a wild strawberry hunt one of your summer musts. Place a berry on the centre of your tongue and let the taste explosion begin.

HARVESTING HAPPINESS

**233** Tea tastes so much lovelier when made with fresh, rather than dried, herbs and flowers. Pop seasonal herbs into these four steaming mugs. Use the seasonal suggestions here or add your own.

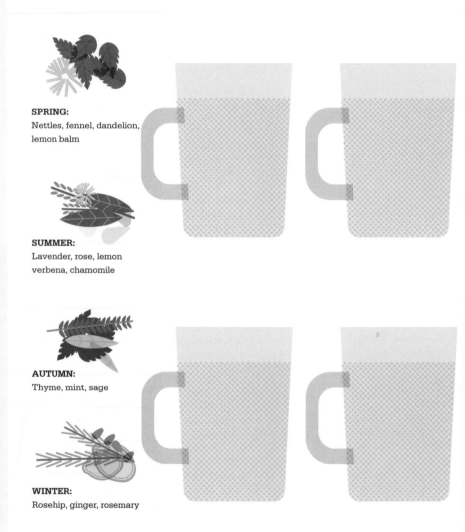

**SPRING:**
Nettles, fennel, dandelion, lemon balm

**SUMMER:**
Lavender, rose, lemon verbena, chamomile

**AUTUMN:**
Thyme, mint, sage

**WINTER:**
Rosehip, ginger, rosemary

**234** Natural foods give off their scent when they are ripe – the natural sugars are at their peak, bringing sweetness to the food's flavour and aroma. Smell an unripe piece of fruit. Smell it again when it is ripe. **Does anything happen to your tongue or mouth as you smell?**

**235** Nothing gives greater joy than foraging for blackberries. At summer's height when days feel slow and stretched – just too sunny for comfort – it's a gift to disappear beneath the canopy of woodland seeking juicy fruits ripe for the plucking. Wander less trodden paths, where the fruits will be all the sweeter for your labour.

**236** Have a blackberry glut? Make ink. Crush a handful of blackberries until they release all of their vibrant juice, strain through a muslin and mix the liquid with a teaspoon of vinegar and a pinch of salt to set the colour and aid preservation. Fashion a writing quill from a found feather: snip the end off to make a clean point. Dip into the ink, and off you go.

*Polish up your calligraphic skills with these flowing fonts.*

*Blackberries*

*Blackberries*

*Blackberries*

HARVESTING HAPPINESS

**237** Come the first days of autumn, bring joy to your winter larder by preserving summer's vibrant goodness. Fruit and veggie gluts – squash, tomatoes, apples and plums – can be preserved in many ways, from jams, jellies and compotes, to fermented krauts, kimchi and pickles.

*Fill these jars with summer's richest pickings.*

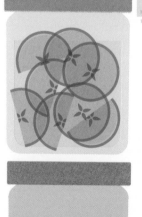

**238** A prize for autumn foragers, mushrooms are nature's very own radical recyclers, taking whatever is in the soil and putting it to good growing use.

**239** Keep a cotton bag in your freezer and add your scraps to it whenever you're preparing veg. The next time you make stock for soup, simply tip the contents into the pot, saving time, effort and money.

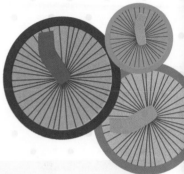

**240** In many cultures, offerings are made at harvest time to thank Mother Earth for her bounty.

*Create a harvest offering here, to celebrate autumn's abundance.*

**241** Hardy plants are a gift for the amateur gardener. Herbs such as thyme, oregano, chives, parsley and mint flourish freely. Though they tend to die back in winter, when grown indoors it's possible to keep them going all-year round. A windowsill is ideal.

**242** We tend to think about food in terms of nutritional value, rather than the qualities, textures and aromas it possesses. Enjoy a meal by thinking about why it is good – is it sweet, sour, salty, pungent, bitter, astringent? Is it dry and rough, or smooth and silken? Bringing awareness to your food heightens your appreciation and joy, too.

**243** Audrey Hepburn said that to plant a garden is to believe in tomorrow. What do you want tomorrow's garden to look like?

*Sow the seeds of intention here.*

.................................................................
.................................................................
.................................................................
.................................................................
.................................................................
.................................................................
.................................................................
.................................................................
.................................................................

**244** These ten commonly wasted veggie and fruit scraps are as useful as they are tasty. By adding unfamiliar and frugal flourishes to your everyday food, you up the nutritional benefits as well as the deliciousness quotient.

**APPLE SKIN** is high in natural pectin, making it ideal for jam-making.

**ORANGE SKIN** can be candied and added to baked goods.

**FENNEL FRONDS** make the most delicious fresh tea.

**HERBY STALKS** such as parsley and coriander are great in soups and stocks.

**CARROT TOPS** have a grassy, sweet flavour; they are brilliant whizzed up with garlic and basil to make pesto.

**CELERY LEAVES** are sweet and tender; they're delicious in juices, salads, soups and stocks.

**BEETROOT LEAVES** are similar to Swiss chard; wilt with butter or olive oil and a pinch of sea salt.

Stir-fry **BROCCOLI STALKS** with garlic, ginger, soy sauce and sesame oil.

**LEEK** and **SPRING ONION** cuttings add brilliant flavour to stock.

Pair **POTATO PEELINGS** with rapeseed oil and sea salt, and roast in the oven for crispy skins that you can top or dip.

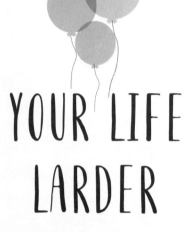

# YOUR LIFE LARDER

**IT'S TIME TO REALISE JUST HOW
RICH YOUR LIFE ALREADY IS**

The immensely profitable world of self-
improvement displays one critical caveat
– the idea that everything can be better if
only we work hard enough to change it. We
live with the constant notion that life is one
long journey to betterment – to do more,
earn more, achieve more . . . to be more.
Rarely do we step off the prefabricated
wheel for long enough to question whether
or not happiness (or the next pay rise, house
move, relationship) really is just around the

next corner, or whether we keep missing it because we fail to see all the wonders that are right in front of our very eyes at any given moment. Well, that's no way to live. Because we might just find that the life we have, and everything in it – the friendships, hobbies, passions, travels and interests – is pretty exciting, and that the skills we have already honed, from being a wonderful listener to a dab hand with a paintbrush, are rather fantastic too. And, when we live in a state of gratitude for all that we already are, and have, the entire axis of our life shifts – from one where we must not rest until we reach where we are going, to one where we get to slow, stop and smell the roses that already line our path, every single day. Being grateful also goes hand-in-hand with another shift in mindset: the ability to stop living beyond our means. To reclaim a joyful mindset, you need to begin by celebrating all of the amazing qualities, attributes, skills and traits you possess right now. And that's precisely what we'll be doing here, in this chapter, with lots of fun, positive, creative prompts to help you identify your strengths and abundant blessings.

**245** A lovely way for you to begin assessing your own strengths is for you to fill these jumbo-sized jars with all of your amazing gifts. From singing to crocheting, letter-writing to listening, dig as deep as you can to unearth your unique talents.

**246** Write down five things that you enjoy doing, but think you are not good at. Irrespective of whether you are, or are not, 'good', consider how you'd feel if you could never do these things again. Make these your reasons to enjoy them as often as you can.

**1.** ......................................................................................................................

**2.** ......................................................................................................................

**3.** ......................................................................................................................

**4.** ......................................................................................................................

**5.** ......................................................................................................................

**247** Many of us spend more time meeting and considering the needs of others, than those of ourselves. For the span of one day, place one mark below for each time you do something for someone else, and a mark for each time you do something for yourself. **Does the balance need to be redressed?**

**248** What do you feel most thankful for in this very moment?

**249** Do you always have to be right? Or do you find it hard to speak up at all? Use this mind map to confront a time when you should have walked away from an argument for the peace of your own mind. Or, use it to confront a time when you should have argued your point.

*How did you feel? What do you wish you had done differently? What can you learn from revisiting it?*

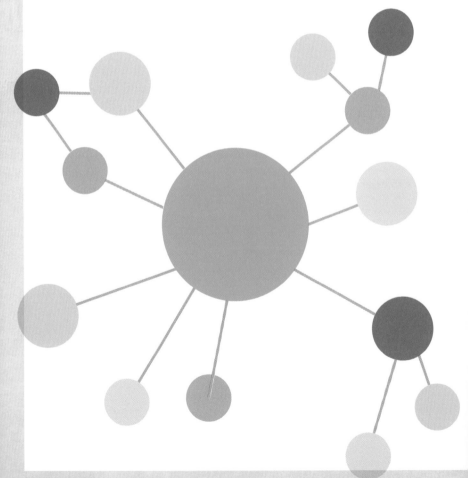

**250** Sometimes, sacrifices are well worth making. Think back on a time when you put everything on the line, or gave up something important, and gained something better as a result. Remind yourself that sometimes we must leave things behind in order to get where we need to go.

**251** Courage is not fearlessness, it is feeling the fear and doing it anyway. Award yourself this medal for bravery.

*Mark it with a time you faced — and conquered — your fear.*

**252** Imagine finding an old school report filled with glowing praise of you as a child.

*Write in all that you wish you had heard back then, here, now.*

**253** How do you respond when complimented? Do you bat it away, make light of it or simply fail to really believe it? Spend time practising how you will respond to a compliment next time – with grace, gratitude and self-belief.

**254** Remember, in the words of **George Eliot**, that it is never too late to be who you might have been. What lights up your soul? What excites you? What do you feel most impassioned and motivated by? Make that the seed of your next project.

**255** Who has been a good friend to you in this lifetime? To whom have you been a good friend? Remember to reach out, not only to value and thank your friends for all they do for you, but for what you do, too – for others and for yourself.

**256** When did you last laugh until you cried?
*Colour in these happy tears.*

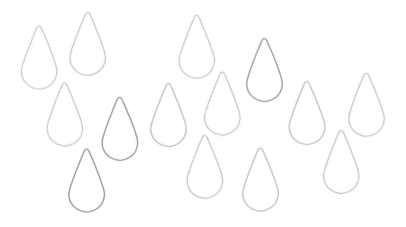

YOUR LIFE LARDER

**257** Everyone has a special gift . . . but some people need a little more help in locating it. Imagine that you are talking to a best friend. What would they say to you when you express a lack of talent?

*List your pep talk points down here.*

..................................................    ..................................................
..................................................    ..................................................
..................................................    ..................................................
..................................................    ..................................................
..................................................    ..................................................
..................................................    ..................................................
..................................................    ..................................................
..................................................    ..................................................
..................................................    ..................................................
..................................................    ..................................................
..................................................    ..................................................
..................................................    ..................................................
..................................................    ..................................................
..................................................    ..................................................

**258** Did you ever keep a journal or a diary? If you did, make the time to read over some of your old entries. It is remarkable how often our lives repeat themselves, how the same questions, doubts, fears come up. But also, how much can change, and so dramatically, within just a short space of time. Remember that the course of your life is determined not by what you think, but by what you act upon.

*What will you act upon tomorrow?*

259 Fill this trophy cabinet with all the times you felt most joyful, free and at peace in yourself. Let this be what you celebrate, irrespective of outcome.

**260** If you were a **sound**, what would you be?

**261** If you were a **colour**, what would you be?

**262** If you were a **taste**, what would you be?

**263** When was the last time you were so immersed in a creative activity that you lost all track of time? It's called 'flow' when the act you engage in absorbs your whole focus; the root of joy. **Do more of it.**

**264** Ninety per cent of women believe themselves to be unphotogenic. Why are we made to believe this? Why do so many of us fear the lens? Find one photograph of yourself that you absolutely love – a photo where you are happy and at ease. **That is you, Beautiful!**

*Make a copy of it and stick it in here.*

**265** Some people like to reward themselves with gifts as incentives for reaching a goal.

*Create your goal (and gift) here.*

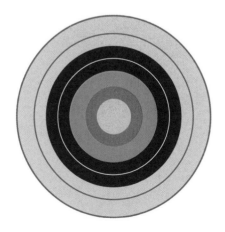

**266** What promise did you make to yourself recently that you failed to keep? Write it down and re-make it, setting a date and time when you can follow through.

.................................................

.................................................

.................................................

.................................................

.................................................

.................................................

.................................................

.................................................

**267** If eyes are the windows to the soul, what would yours express with one look?

*Have fun adding detail to these portal-like eyes.*

**268** Write your name down the side of this page. Now create an acrostic by starting a new word with each of the letters in your name. Choose skills and traits to celebrate – for example, **MIA: MUSICAL; INVENTIVE; ARTISTIC.**

**269** Create a fun motto that sums you up and 'print' it on this T-shirt. Imagine wearing it with pride.

**270** Many of us hold on to things that weigh us down – from the scratchy shirt we never feel comfortable in to old photographs from troubling times.

*Fill these hopeful balloons with the things you no longer need and then cut them loose.*

**271** Let your mind loose with a 'wonder word search'. Fill the grid with ten words that describe you, then enter random letters in the other squares. Come back to this page on a day when you need reminding of your inherent wonder and complete the word search. Colour in your 'wonder words' in the brightest ink.

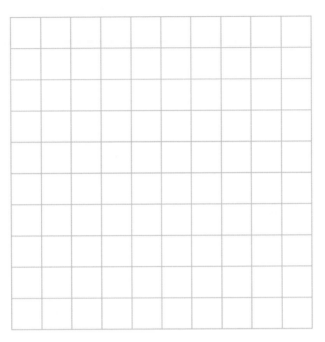

**272** What is your favourite item of clothing? What item of clothing do you wear most? There should be no distinction.

*Sketch your favourite garment here and then hang it out, ready to wear tomorrow.*

*273* What makes
your heart sing?

*Fill this heart up to the brim
with things you love.*

*274* How often do we say **'I can't do this'**,
and then do it anyway?

*Have fun crossing out these joy-stealing space invaders.
Every time you cancel out an 'I can't', replace it with an 'I can!'.*

**275** Imagine that you are about to graduate from the school of your life. What qualifications have you earned along your life's path – from resilience to humour, resourcefulness to kindness?

*Add them to your graduation certificate.*

YOUR LIFE LARDER

# BEGIN AGAIN

**IF WE LIVED A LIFE WITHOUT MISTAKES, WE'D LEARN VERY LITTLE**

Human beings are quite incredible – inherently resilient, innovative and adaptable. We have so much to be proud of – we learned how to make fire and invented the wheel, after all. Yet there are countless times in our lives when we let our own self-limiting beliefs sneak in and fool us into suspecting that we aren't as good as we ought to be, times when we let comparison, doubt and fear steal our magical thunder and hold us back from living the life we want. Yes, we all have our fair share of dirty laundry – stuff that's been hanging around for years: regrets, memories, fear, guilt. No one is immune from making mistakes, but there is no shame in this. The 'beginner's mind', a Zen Buddhist ideology, refers to the open, receptive, ever-learning state of being that accepts we are not experts (and are never going to be), that we are all eternal students, here to experience life moment by moment without set expectations or rigid mindsets. Isn't that freeing? To realise that wherever we come from, whatever we have done and however many mistakes we fear we have made in our lives, that not one of us is immune from the opportunity to move on and move forward. Here, we reclaim our joy by getting out of our own way, by renouncing our need to be always right and by understanding that the more fixed our mindset is, the more limited our potential becomes. Carrying around a lifetime of guilt, worry, fear and regret? This is where you can sketch out and doodle down all of our perceived imperfections and inconsistencies, and clear the air once and for all.

**276** Air your dirty laundry on this imaginary washing line. Write down the old regrets you want to 'wash away'. Imagine popping all of the items into the machine and seeing them come out in the wash.

........................................................................

........................................................................

........................................................................

........................................................................

........................................................................

........................................................................

........................................................................

........................................................................

........................................................................

........................................................................

**277** Imagine putting all of your newly washed 'laundry' back in your wardrobe.

*Line these shelves with fresh intentions —
from the highest priorities to the lesser ones.*

**278** The beliefs we hold about ourselves define us in many ways. What beliefs might be holding you back?

*Write them down here.*

...............................................
...............................................
...............................................
...............................................
...............................................
...............................................
...............................................
...............................................
...............................................
...............................................
...............................................
...............................................
...............................................
...............................................
...............................................
...............................................
...............................................
...............................................
...............................................
...............................................
...............................................
...............................................
...............................................
...............................................

**279** Against each self-limiting belief you wrote in the previous activity, write one way in which you have already disproven it . . . or intend to. Remember, thoughts are just thoughts; they are not facts.

...............................................
...............................................
...............................................
...............................................
...............................................
...............................................
...............................................
...............................................
...............................................
...............................................
...............................................
...............................................
...............................................
...............................................
...............................................
...............................................
...............................................
...............................................
...............................................
...............................................
...............................................
...............................................
...............................................
...............................................

**280** **Carl Jung** said, 'What you resist not only persists, but will grow in size.' Grab the scariest, most shameful, best-hidden skeleton in your closet with both hands.

*What do you want to say to it?*
*What does it want to say back?*

...................................................
...................................................
...................................................
...................................................
...................................................
...................................................
...................................................
...................................................
...................................................
...................................................
...................................................
...................................................
...................................................
...................................................
...................................................

**281** An open mind comes from a desire to be curious. Instead of responding to situations with certainty – 'I know how this works' – are there times when you would be better served by responding with **'I wonder how this works?'**.

**282** We often feel we must master a new skill quickly in order to be seen as successful. All you need to do to master a new skill is not give up. You may fall down ten times, but if you get up eleven times, you have still succeeded.

*Name a skill that you have given up on but could return to one more time.*

**283** Have fun solving this word code with a beginner's mind. Ask yourself, **'I wonder how this works?'** Take as long as you need. No prizes for winning – only trying.

Only three of the following four words has a number code. If the letters correspond to numbers, what is the number code for the word **MUSE**?

You'll find the answer 184.

SWUM

7236

FERN

1687

WEST

8139

TRUE

**284** Colour in this technicolour butterfly as a reminder of the feeling you want to shake off today, then vigorously flap your arms and body to release the sensation from your physical being.

**285** Rosemary is a wonderful aromatic herb, long associated with remembrance. Paint up this pretty pot with rosemary sprigs, as a reminder of someone special you want to hold close in your memory.

**286** Begin writing a new diary entry where all of the negative narratives from the past year work out wonderfully well in the end. Keep coming back and adding to it each time you imagine twists and turns in your own happily ending tale.

**287** It is a sad truth that unkind comments tend to linger longer than kind ones. Make a point of writing down any unkind comments you wish to forget here, in pencil.

*Now erase them all and write over them with kind comments.*

**288** In Sanskrit, mandala means 'circle' and these intricate circular patterns symbolise our own inherent 'completeness': we are all whole and we are all one. Used as meditation tools, mandalas are beautiful to draw yourself.

*To get you in the mood, let your pens loose on these beautiful mandalas.*

**289** Just like waves and clouds, difficult times will come and go.

*Add washes of colour to this fleeting, changeable scene as a reminder of the inherent impermanence of everything.*

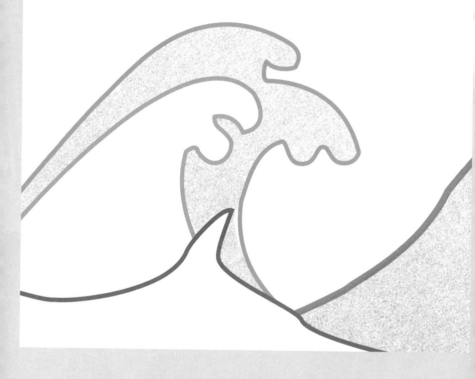

**290** If you could live your life by any motto, what would it be? **Ask yourself what's stopping you.**

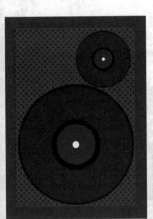

**291** Was there a cheery song you used to play or sing, when the going got tough?

*Write the lyrics down in the space above.*

189

**292** Trace around your hand. Then, focusing on the palm of your hand, sketch in the clearest lines you can see. Imagine that each one developed as a result of the life you have lived.

*Name each line and give it a story.*

**293** Imagine drinking 'truth juice'. Now you have no choice but to say precisely what you are thinking, all day long.

*Write the thoughts you want to remember on the bottle here.*

**294** Living life in full technicolour means never dimming your own personality, but living your whole, unapologetic truth. Fill in this swatch chart with your heart and soul's boldest colours. Then give every colour a name that is unique and meaningful to you.

**295** Stick in a picture of someone or something that upsets you.

*Let loose with the black marker pen. Don't worry — no one will ever see!*

**296** We might all do well to take a leaf out of a child's book – they're far too busy having fun to care what others think of them. Close your eyes and re-imagine yourself as a kid, wild and free, marching to the beat of your own drum. Hold that feeling in your heart!

**297** You needn't wait until New Year to set your intentions and resolutions. The simple act of choosing a word for the day can help you get clear on what it is you want to feel and achieve. Etch your word into this calendar each morning for a week. Every time you lose your way, repeat the word in your mind to create both clarity and purpose.

| M | | |
|---|---|---|
| T | | |
| W | | |
| T | | |
| F | | |
| S | | |
| S | | |

**298** Take a deep breath in and then exhale for as long as you can, until you feel that your lungs are completely empty. Do this every time there is a weight in your chest that you want to lift.

**299** Make a soothing oil to smell each time you feel anxious. Add five drops each of lavender, rose and geranium oil to a small 10ml bottle or vial. Top up with sweet almond, sunflower or coconut oil. Shake to mix. Dab a drop of the oil onto pulse points and inhale deeply as often as needed.

**300** Laughter yoga is a modern form of yoga that involves long periods of voluntary laughter. Shake your body and limbs for five minutes to loosen and warm up. Now begin 'laughing' by repeating 'ho ho ha ha ha' and smiling. Repeat until the urge to laugh comes over you. It's a wonderful antidote to a stressful day.

*Try it!*

**301** There's an old saying that when the gods wish to punish us, they grant our wishes. What things have you dreamed of, only to realise they are not as wonderful as you imagined them to be? Do not chastise yourself – we are all made to have wants and aspirations – but we are, in fact, most content when we fully cherish all that we already have. Begin where you are.

**302** Remember that even the gods get it wrong sometimes. What dreams have you had that have come true and brought great joy with them?

*Celebrate them here.*

303 Where do you hold your worry? For some people it's in the neck and shoulders, for others it's in the stomach or the jaw. Imagine speaking to this part of your body with kindness and acceptance. Tell yourself that it's OK to let go of the tension, that the past is in the past and that nothing beyond the nanosecond of the 'now' exists anyway.

**304** Let's exercise our 'beginner's mind'. Reflect on a time when you went into a situation with a completely open mind. **What was the outcome?**

Now, reflect on a time when you went into a situation with a closed mindset, full of assumptions. **What was this outcome?**

..................................................
..................................................
..................................................
..................................................
..................................................
..................................................
..................................................
..................................................
..................................................
..................................................
..................................................
..................................................
..................................................
..................................................
..................................................
..................................................
..................................................
..................................................
..................................................
..................................................
..................................................
..................................................
..................................................
..................................................

..................................................
..................................................
..................................................
..................................................
..................................................
..................................................
..................................................
..................................................
..................................................
..................................................
..................................................
..................................................
..................................................
..................................................
..................................................
..................................................
..................................................
..................................................
..................................................
..................................................

# YOUR JOY BOX

**DON'T SAVE THOSE DREAMS
FOR A RAINY DAY**

Everyone should have a joy box: a place in
the home to keep things that always cheer
you up, make you smile and remind you of
golden memories. It can be both a physical
space to store, celebrate and cherish good
stuff, and a spiritual, mental and emotional
one – a way of cherishing and giving
thanks for all the good things in your life.
In my home, I have a box that looks like
a large old book, gifted to me by a friend.
It sits on my bookshelf, nestled among all
the other books. But when I take it down
and open the 'front cover', inside are

postcards, letters, photographs, cuttings
and keepsakes – my life's little treasures.
If I am feeling nostalgic, I may spend an
hour sitting on the floor of my bedroom, re-
reading each one, poring over the pictures,
lost on a merry jaunt down memory lane. I
make a point of adding really funny things
to the box, too. My box reminds me of the
stuff that really matters: friendship, love,
laughter. And, if I've been feeling a little
directionless, it steers me back on course,
guiding me to make more time for friends,
to have more of my own joyful adventures
and to make choices that will lift my spirit
and fill my heart. Here, you'll find gentle,
intentional nudges to help steer your ship
along life's happier shores – places where
self-care, jubilation, levity and wonder are
in abundance and where, when you take
the time to stop, kick off your shoes and
dive into the waters, you remember what it
feels like to truly come home.

**305** Make time over the coming months to start your own joy box. If you have memories and mementos scattered about your home, gather any you do not wish to display. Find, decorate or repurpose a box in a way that encapsulates joy for you.

*Take great joy in adding to your box each and every time something touches your heart.*

**306** What craft did you enjoy most at school? Making collages or papier mâché? Knitting or woodwork? Watercolours or appliqué? Add touches of your lost arts to your joy box – whether directly to the box itself or stored within – as an ongoing project to pick up on rainy days.

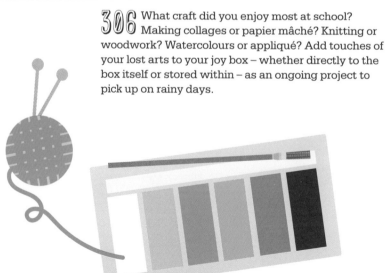

**307** Imagine your heart is its own joy box and that each time something kind, positive or hopeful happens, a little more joy feeds into the space in your chest. One of the best ways to grow this inner glow is by practising gratitude. Don't let lovely things go unacknowledged – **WITNESS** them, **FEEL** them, **GIVE THANKS** for them.

**308** Imagine your joy as the liquid in a cup.
What choices fill the cup? What choices empty it?

**309** Write down three ways in which you can honour the filling of your cup.

*Make it happen.*

1.

2.

3.

**310** Create a happy haiku – a three-line poem with five, then seven, then five syllables – celebrating a cup-filling pastime.

**311** What's the oddest and most unlikely thing you would save for your joy box?

..............................................
..............................................
..............................................
..............................................
..............................................
..............................................
..............................................
..............................................
..............................................
..............................................
..............................................
..............................................
..............................................
..............................................
..............................................
..............................................

**312** Maya Angelou once said: '... **people will forget what you said, people will forget what you did, but people will never forget how you made them feel'.** How can you choose to live your life today, in ways that will leave a trail of loveliness in your wake?

..............................................
..............................................
..............................................
..............................................
..............................................
..............................................
..............................................
..............................................
..............................................
..............................................
..............................................
..............................................

**313** Close your eyes. Imagine you are walking somewhere, perhaps on a path, or traversing a field or forest. Imagine that each time your foot touches the earth, a new bloom or blossom springs up. As you walk, repeat to yourself: **'I leave loveliness in my wake.'**

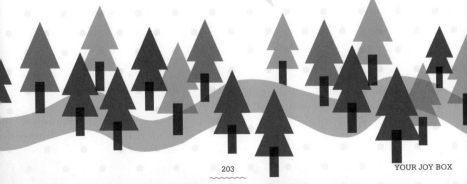

YOUR JOY BOX

**314** Copy or scan and print out a selection of favourite photographs, notes and mementos.

*Make a spirit-lifting collage with them here.*

## 315 Stick an extra-special picture here, in this Polaroid frame.

*Add a caption that says it all.*

**316** **'Urgent'** is a matter of life or death. It is act now, or else. Yet we mark our emails with the word, and letters stamped with it regularly fly through our letterboxes. This is because we are hardwired to act when something truly IS urgent. Companies take advantage of this and use it to get our attention. Let's take that power back. Spend a few minutes thinking about the things you have labeled 'urgent' that are not, in fact, a matter of life or death. Add them to the 'Not actually urgent' list below.

**NOT ACTUALLY URGENT!!!**

**317** Do you have a favourite recipe that a friend or family member cooks for you, but you cannot make yourself? Ask them to share the recipe with you and add it to your joy box. Make it when you need reminding of the special bond you share.

**318** Taste and smell have the ability to transport us back to past memories with such power and precision. What 'taste' would you add to your joy box? What smell? Think about things that combine both, too, such as childhood sweets.

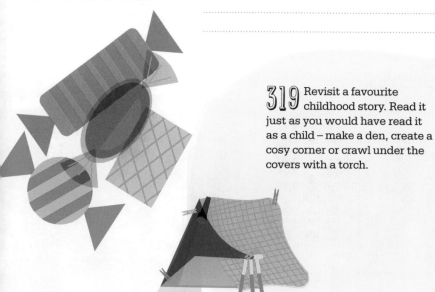

**319** Revisit a favourite childhood story. Read it just as you would have read it as a child – make a den, create a cosy corner or crawl under the covers with a torch.

**320** Besides the special and meaningful things in your joy box, make a point of displaying things that bring you joy where you can see them all the time.

**321** Create a small shrine in your favourite room, to display whatever your heart is most drawn to that day. Things to add might include something from nature (a feather, dried flower or pinecone), something made by a loved one, something that glistens, glows or vibrates (a candle, crystal or small singing bowl). You may want to use a pretty tray to contain your choices.

*Begin planning your own simple shrine, here.*

**322** Was there something a loved one in your life used to do whenever you needed cheering up?

*Create your own mind map, filled with joyful gestures that never failed to put a smile on your face.*

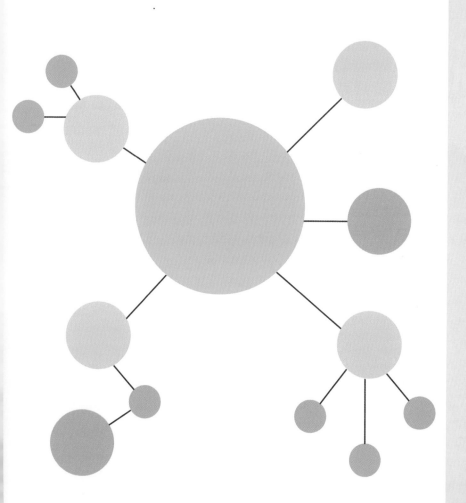

**323** Add a joyful gesture to a day in your diary as a treat to enjoy later in the week.

**324** Small victories should be celebrated. From changing a lightbulb to hanging a picture, no job is too small for a pat on the back.

**325** Some of the best dreams are the simplest ones. Set yourself five tiny, everyday wishes and hopes to remind yourself of the joyful, generous potential within ready reach.

*Make a list of your wishes here.*

1. ........................................................

2. ........................................................

3. ........................................................

4. ........................................................

5. ........................................................

**326** What was the last bit of good news you received that made you want to skip around the room?

*Close your eyes and let the memory of it fill you up.*

**327** Make your joy box a special place to store future gifts for others. Don't forgo the joy of picking up a thoughtful postcard, simply because you don't have the right recipient yet. By placing an item of beauty in your box, you create an opportunity to share your joy with another in the future.

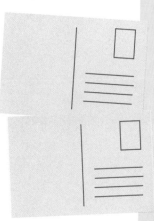

**328** Save beautiful offcuts of wrapping paper, fabric, wallpaper and the fronts of pleasing greetings cards in a special envelope that fits inside your joy box. They're great for fashioning gift tags and labels for friends.

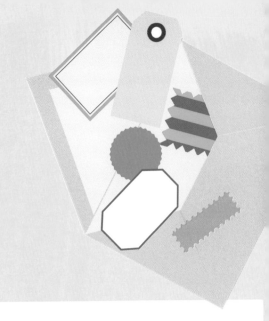

**329** Fewer than half of us print photographs anymore. Tip this trend by spending a quiet hour selecting a handful of special images on your phone. Print them out and display them in a frame, the good old-fashioned way.

**330** Often, we tune into songs without really registering their lyrics, yet our subconscious may make a connection that means something to us. If a song keeps popping into your mind, but you're not sure what the lyrics are, look them up. What do they reveal?

**331** It can be helpful to tap along your ribcage with a closed fist, whenever you want to calm down or release pent-up frustration. As you do so, imagine the ball of worry or anger dissipating with each tap – like a balloon of hot water dispersing into smaller, cooler droplets, which then evaporate entirely.

**332** Snip nourishing and delicious recipes out of magazines and decide on one evening a week when you will actually enjoy them. Keep the recipes that you truly love and enjoy in your joy box.

333 Keep a small stash of art and craft supplies in your joy box so that you have all you need in one place to create a meditative moment. Tangle art is a great way to begin – it's a simple way to create beautiful, repeating patterns that are as pleasing to draw as they are to look at. You simply repeat your 'tangle' pattern over and over, rotating the page each time, until you have filled the intended space – usually a simple square or circle.

*Try sketching a simple 'tangle' below.*

**334** Make a promise to yourself that you will not save your favourite things 'for best'. Ask yourself, 'Am I not good enough to enjoy my best things, every day?' Every day is a special occasion – you are alive! That's worth celebrating!

# THE PLAY LIST

Adulting isn't always all it's cracked up
to be. Even for those who live a relatively
low-key life, we must still navigate our
collective eco-anxiety and global social-
political unrest and uncertainty. The
cumulative effect of life's daily challenges
– exacerbated by, among other things,
24/7 connectivity and technology – has
brought many of us to the point where
we feel continually overwhelmed and
constantly stressed. And this is why we
need a monumentally magnificent dose of
joy to mitigate it! There is nothing more
life-affirming than joy – joy that roots itself
down into the foundations of real life and

sprouts up, blooming and beautiful, through every seam of our everyday fabric. Here, in this chapter, we take our lead from children, who are naturally joyous, curious, free-spirited. We remember how to learn through play, where every day is a rich, enjoyable adventure. Though it is not easy to free ourselves from years of being told to grow up and stop being so silly, there is ample research to show that having a playful state of mind not only reduces stress levels, but also makes us more creative and adaptable in our responses and solutions to stressful situations. In fact 'play' is quite possibly the most underrated pastime of all, as it leads to improved wellbeing, better relationships, increased longevity and a better night's sleep, among other things. Here, we banish the rules and regulations and the to-do lists, and just return to some good old-fashioned fun. From the simple joy of a good tongue twister to the naughtiest tricks we ever played, this chapter is filled with celebratory ways to coax out your inner kid.

**335** A steamed-up window is a playful invitation to get creative with a bit of doodling. Free your inner artist (and big kid) and remember those simple childhood pastimes.

*Repeat your doodle here.*

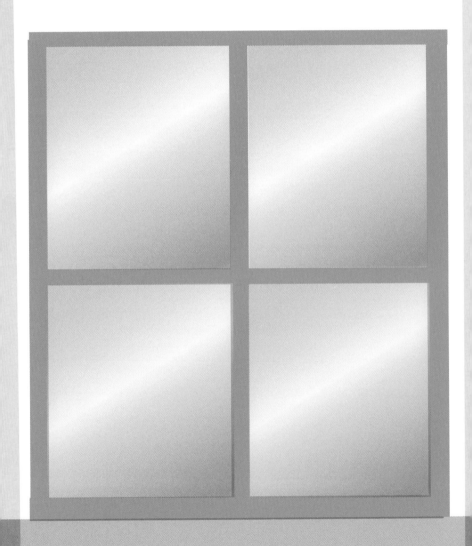

# 336

Write a letter to yourself as you are now,
from the perspective of yourself as a young child.

*What advice would you offer? What hopes would you share?*

**337** Planes flying overhead always come with rich and imaginative adventure stories.
**Where is this plane going?**
**Who's onboard?**
**What happens once they arrive?**

**338** Have fun saying these three devilishly tricky tongue twisters out loud, speeding up with each repetition. Challenge your friends for bonus joy.

BETTY BOTTER BOUGHT SOME BUTTER
BUT SHE SAID THE BUTTER'S BITTER
IF I PUT IT IN MY BATTER, IT WILL MAKE MY BATTER BITTER
BUT A BIT OF BETTER BUTTER WILL MAKE MY BATTER BETTER
SO 'TWAS BETTER BETTY BOTTER BOUGHT A BIT OF BETTER BUTTER

THE SIXTH SICK SHEIK'S SIXTH SHEEP'S SICK

A TUTOR WHO TOOTED THE FLUTE TRIED TO TUTOR TWO TOOTERS TO TOOT. SAID THE TWO TO THE TUTOR, 'IS IT HARDER TO TOOT OR TO TUTOR TWO TOOTERS TO TOOT?'

**339** Did you ever have a special 'spell' you'd repeat as a child? Something to comfort you or make you feel powerful, or to change what was happening around you?

*Write down the words that come to you now.*

......................................................................................

......................................................................................

......................................................................................

......................................................................................

......................................................................................

......................................................................................

......................................................................................

**340** When you were a child, too young to know about careers, what did you aspire to be? A unicorn? An explorer? A superhero?

*Draw your childhood hero/ine here.*

**341** Make a natural botanical print. Place leaves and flowers over a piece of plain fabric and layer a second piece of fabric over them. Using a hammer, tap on each plant and flower until the pigment comes through the top fabric. Carefully peel the top layer away, and let the leaves and flowers dry before peeling them gently away.

*How will you use your fantastic botanical print fabric?*

**342** Unbelievably, 242 words can be made from the word **UNBELIEVABLE!**

*Challenge yourself to come up with as many as you can over time.*

UNBELIEVABLE

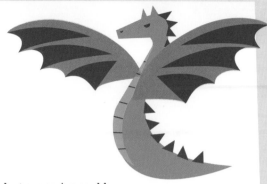

**343** As children, even the simplest scenarios could
be made magical, such is the power of imagination.
The next time you find yourself queuing with little to do,
imagine something remarkable happening – a dragon landing;
a SWAT team storming in; a witch casting a wonderful spell.
Play the story out as far as it will go.

**344** Children see treasure
in the most throwaway
things: bottle tops, bits of string,
sticky tack. Fill this pocket with
the things you collected as a kid.
Remember how each felt to hold,
marvel at it and recall the sorts of
things you'd use it for.

........................................

........................................

........................................

........................................

........................................

........................................

........................................

........................................

........................................

........................................

........................................

........................................

........................................

**345** What was the most mischievous thing you did as a kid? Re-live it here, guilt-free.

**346** What was your favourite sweet from the sweetshop?

*Draw it here.*

**347** Remember when cereal boxes used to come with toys inside, and with stories and puzzles on the box? Good times!

*Design your own cereal box here. What gift would you find inside?*

**348** Imagine having five vouchers from friends and family members that you can use to get anything you want. What would they do for you?

*Fill them in here.*

**349** What was the first film you saw at the cinema? What do you remember about it?

**350** Rolling down hills, jumping off walls, climbing trees… adults tend to think of these things as a bit risky, yet children don't think twice about such natural play. When was the last time you experienced a thrill of breathless excitement?

**351** Treat yourself to an impromptu song and dance whenever you find yourself home alone. Close the windows and let those vocal chords loose!

**352** Peace activist and writer **Satish Kumar** created the Pilgrim's Formula as a guide for contentment. It is where we live five per cent in the past, fifteen per cent in the future, and eighty per cent in the present moment. This is where most children live – it comes naturally. Consider how you can re-frame your focus and thoughts to move closer to this joy-supporting formula.

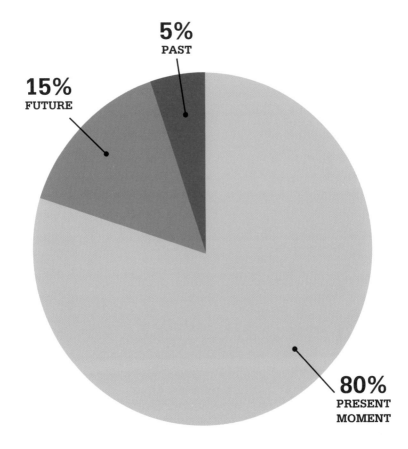

**5%**
PAST

**15%**
FUTURE

**80%**
PRESENT
MOMENT

**353** Stuck on a decision? Ask yourself: what would so-and-so do? From bonkers to brave, silly to sage, have fun putting yourself into your childhood hero or heroine's shoes . . . what would the outcome be?

..............................................
..............................................
..............................................
..............................................
..............................................
..............................................
..............................................
..............................................
..............................................
..............................................
..............................................

**354** Time to unleash your imaginary friend. What are they called? What would they do and say? How would they behave?

*Draw your friend here.*

**355** Fall back in love with lists, replacing dull duties with playful joys.

*Use the following themes to get you started.*

### FIVE AWESOME POP SONGS

..................................................
..................................................
..................................................
..................................................
..................................................

### FIVE BEST SUMMER HOLIDAYS

..................................................
..................................................
..................................................
..................................................
..................................................

### FIVE FAVOURITE ICE-CREAM FLAVOURS

..................................................
..................................................
..................................................
..................................................
..................................................

### FIVE COOLEST FICTIONAL CHARACTERS

..................................................
..................................................
..................................................
..................................................
..................................................

**356** Rainbows and unicorns, witches and warriors – which characters and motifs always made it into your stories? **Why do you think they did?**

**357** Flash fiction is hugely entertaining – a super-short story, in which an entire world is encapsulated in **just a few hundred words**. Don't waste time or words on the introduction, but begin right in the middle of the story, choose every word wisely and make sure the final line packs a punch.

*Off you go . . .*

**358** Challenge yourself to microfiction – where an entire story is **fifty words or less** – using the story you wrote in the previous activity.

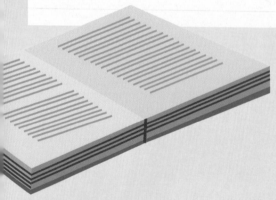

**359** Before we learned to read in our heads, we all read out loud. Re-embrace the joy of reading out loud with a book of favourite poetry or prose.

**360** A child will often greet the onset of rain with a joyful 'it's raining!', overtaken with the urge to run out and get soaked. Grab your next chance to dance or run around in the rain . . . and follow it up with a warm bath and cosy cuppa.

**361** Children are often chided with **'look, don't touch'**, but their urge to hold and feel things is intrinsic to learning. We often realise things about objects only when we hold them – a soft, fluffy thing may feel surprisingly rough, while a scaled, leathery surface might be deliciously soft. Move around your home, or outside space, picking up objects at random. Learn their secrets as you cup them in your hands.

*Draw your favourite discoveries here.*

**362** Whatever you find completely hilarious – from sarcastic memes on the internet to re-runs of quality sitcoms – carve out a slice of time to binge on them, laughing out loud until your sides hurt.

**363** Beginning on the 'start dot', complete an impromptu, unplanned drawing, without lifting your pencil from the page until you reach the 'end dot'.

START

●

●

END

**364** Taste combinations to love or hate: **ham and pineapple; peanut butter and marmite; chocolate and banana.**

*Add three of your weirdest childhood favourites to the mix.*

**365** Add details to this rosette and award it to your inner kid for making it through another day with a hearty dose of fun and frolics.

## Further Resources

# BOOKS

### ABOUT HAPPINESS,
### PLAY & FLOW

1 *The Joy Journal for Magical Everyday Play: Easy Activities & Creative Craft for Kids and their Grown-ups*, Laura Brand (Bluebird, 2020)

2 *Play: How It Shapes the Brain, Opens the Imagination, and Invigorates the Soul*, Stuart Brown M.D. (Penguin, 2010)

3 *Flow, The Psychology of Optimal Experience*, Mihaly Csikszentmihalyi (HarperCollins, 2008)

4 *Man's Search for Meaning*, Viktor E. Frankl (Beacon Press, 2019)

5 *The Art of Happiness: A Handbook for Living*, The Dalai Lama and Howard C Cutler (Hodder, 1999)

6 *Joyful: The Surprising Power of Ordinary Things to Create Extraordinary Happiness*, Ingrid Fetell Lee (Rider, 2018)

7 *Happiness: Essential Mindfulness Practices*, Thich Nhat Hanh (Parallax Press, 2009)

8 *Michael Rosen's Book of Play: Why Play Really Matters, and 101 Ways to Get More of it in Your Life*, Michael Rosen (Wellcome Collection, 2019)

9 *Play the Forest School Way: Woodland Games, Crafts and Skills for Adventurous Kids Book*, Jane Worroll and Peter Houghton (Watkins, 2008)

# BOOKS
## ABOUT NATURE &
## SELF-SUFFICIENCY

1 *If Women Rose Rooted: A Life changing Journey to Authenticity and Belonging*, Sharon Blackie (September Publishing, 2019)

2 *100 Things to do in a Forest*, Jennifer Davis and Eleanor Taylor (Laurence King, 2020)

3 *Trees, Leaves, Flowers & Seeds: Visual Encyclopedia of the Plant Kingdom*, DK and The Smithsonian Institution (DK, 2019)

4 *Braiding Sweetgrass: Indigenous Wisdom, Scientific Knowledge and the Teachings of Plants*, Robin Wall Kimmerer (Penguin, 2020)

5 *The Almanac: A Seasonal Guide to 2021*, Lia Leendertz (Mitchell Beazley: 2020)

6 *Food for Free*, Richard Mabey (Collins, 2012)

7 *The New Complete Book of Self-Sufficiency: the Classic Guide for Realists and Dreamers*, John Seymour (DK, 2019)

8 Self-Sufficiency: *Foraging for Wild Foods*, David Squire (IMM Lifestyle, 2015)

9 *Practical Self-Sufficiency: the Complete Guide to Sustainable Living Today*, Dick Strawbridge and James Strawbridge (DK, 2020)

# BOOKS
## ABOUT CREATIVITY
## & STORYTELLING

1 *The Story Cure: An A-Z of Books to Keep Kids Happy, Healthy and Wise*, Ella Berthould and Susan Elderkin (Canongate, 2016)

2 *The Artist's Way: A Spiritual Path to Higher Creativity*, Julia Cameron (Souvenir Press, 2020)

3 *Big Magic: How to Live a Creative Life and Let Go of Your Fear*, Elizabeth Gilbert (Bloomsbury, 2016)

4 *The Storytelling Animal: How Stories Make Us Human*, Jonathan Gottshcall (Houghton Mifflin Harcourt USA 2013)

5 *Creative Confidence: Unleashing the Creative Potential within Us All*, David Kelley and Tom Kelley (HarperCollins, 2015)

6 *The Lost Words and The Lost Spells*, Robert Macfarlane and Jackie Morris (Hamish Hamilton, 2020)

7 *Creatrix: She Who Makes* by Lucy H Pearce (Womancraft Publishing, 2019)

8 *Daemon Voices: Essays on Storytelling*, Philip Pullman (David Fickling Books, 2017)

FURTHER RESOURCES

# Further Resources

## WEBSITE

1. *Action for Happiness*
   actionforhappiness.org

2. *Project Happiness*
   projecthappiness.org

3. *The Conscious Kid*
   theconsciouskid.com

4. *The Happiness Research Institute*
   happinessresearchinstitute.com

5. *The Happy Newspaper*
   thehappynewspaper.com

## MAGAZINES

1. *Oh magazine*
   ohmag.co.uk

2. *Flow*
   www.flowmagazine.com

3. *Juno*
   www.junomagazine.com

4. *Resurgence*
   www.resurgence.org/magazine

5. *The Green Parent*
   thegreenparent.co.uk

6. *The Happy News*
   https://thehappynewspaper.com